"David Young's *Servant Leadership for Church Renewal* is a logical sequel to his earlier book, *A New Heart and a New Spirit*. It is appropriate that his volume on church renewal should be followed by this one on church leadership, since the latter is an indispensable requisite of the former.

"Drawing upon his experience as a pastor and teacher of pastors, the author offers his own thorough, practical, and biblically based perspective on the meaning, implications, and importance of servant leadership. The result should prove to be a useful resource for seminary students, pastors, and lay leaders."
—*Richard Stoll Armstrong, Ashenfelter Professor of Ministry and Evangelism Emeritus, Princeton Theological Seminary*

"David Young combines his years in pastoral ministry, his keen understanding of the role of pastor as leader, and his knowledge gained from research and teaching to produce this excellent book for the church and its leaders. *Servant Leadership for Church Renewal* combines a comprehensive analysis of the role of the pastor as both servant and leader, with a variety of concrete ways in which servant leadership is worked out in the life of the congregation.

"This is a highly recommended read for any pastor seeking to bring renewal to the church through self-renewal and a commitment to a kind of godly leadership that is so needed in the church today."
—*Scott Rodin, President, Eastern Baptist Theological Seminary*

"David Young's material is rooted in solid biblical study and reputable contemporary sources. He puts useful resources in the hands of people with a practical bent. Young takes seriously an Anabaptist believers church theological framework. Participants in his courses here have given quite positive evaluations.

"His book will be a strong stimulus to pastors and congregational leaders in a wide range of settings. It balances content and programming in a flexible and sensitive way. I recommend *Servant Leadership for Church Renewal* for wide use by church leaders."
—*George R. Brunk III, Dean, Eastern Mennonite Seminary*

"David Young shows boundless enthusiasm for spiritual renewal. His deep and personal acquaintance with his subject and his earnest compassion for people create a warm rapport with students. David's presentations have effective references to Scripture, clear and concise outlines, and practical applications and illustrations. I have always been enriched in seminars taught by David Young."
—*Richard Sisco, Pastor, Akron (Pa.) Church of the Brethren*

"When we were developing a church vision, we consulted with David. As he shared his concepts on renewal, I found his relational approach very consistent with how our church functioned. After the initial consultation, all members of the elder team remarked that working with David's structure gave them a sense of hope.

"David was direct, clear, and patient. His ideas made sense to us, his approach was collaborative, and his structure for renewal was flexible. All of this was very compatible with the struggles of a church committed, as we are, to fashioning vision from a servant-leadership perspective. His method was inclusive and open to contextual modification. His time with us was beneficial in helping us to be sensitive to the ministry God is uniquely creating at Frazer Mennonite Church."
—*Jason Kuniholm, Pastor, Frazer (Pa.) Mennonite Church*

Servant Leadership
for
Church Renewal

The Lamb in the midst of the throne
will be their shepherd,
and he will guide them
to springs of living water.

—*Revelation 7:17*

Servant Leadership *for* Church Renewal

Shepherds by the Living Springs

David S. Young

Herald
Press

Scottdale, Pennsylvania
Waterloo, Ontario

Library of Congress Cataloging-in-Publication Data
Young, David S. (David Samuel), 1944-
　　Servant leadership for church renewal : shepherds by the living
　　springs / David S. Young.
　　　　p.　cm.
　　Includes bibliographical references.
　　ISBN 0-8361-9108-0 (alk. paper)
　　　1. Christian leadership. 2. Service (Theology) I. title.
　　BV652.1.Y65　1999
　　253—dc21　　　　　　　　　　　　　　　　　　99-17530

All Scripture is used by permission, all rights reserved, and unless
otherwise specified, is from the *Revised Standard Version Bible*, copyright 1946, 1952, 1971, by the Division of Christian Education of the
National Council of the Churches of Christ in the USA. GNB, from
the *Good News Bible*—Old Testament: copyright © American Bible
Society 1976; New Testament: copyright © American Bible Society
1966, 1971, 1976. NRSV, from the *New Revised Standard Version Bible*,
copyright 1989 by the Division of Christian Education of the
National Council of the Churches of Christ in the USA.

Users of the book are hereby granted permission to copy the
appended "Worksheets" for their own use, but not to sell.

To Joan,
companion, friend, servant,
one who counsels,
"Keep it practical,"
and to the rest of my family:
my mother, for believing in
the project; son Jonathan,
for technical support;
and son Andrew, for
unbounding enthusiasm.

Contents

Foreword

We are living in a time when two of the most rich and defining words of the Christian life—*renewal* and *transformation*—are being rendered meaningless by misuse and abuse. So why another book on church renewal and transformation?

Perhaps because David Young has gotten it so very right! Refusing to abandon this highly spiritual language, Young has filled these tired terms with a vibrancy that inspires while it informs. If the call to ministry is a call to servant leadership, and if the church is the church of the living Christ who *makes all things new*—then this book is a timely challenge and a much-needed inspirational call to every pastor and Christian leader.

In 1986 David Young served as adjunct professor at Eastern Baptist Theological Seminary in Philadelphia, teaching a "Church Renewal" course. From experience in the classroom, added to years in the ministry, Young produced his first book, *A New Heart and a New Spirit: A Plan for Renewing Your Church*. His main text was Psalm 51, and he developed the book around its restoration theme.

He also introduced his own understanding of servant leadership as it emerged from the process of church renewal and transformation. In developing the "servant as leader" as the core of renewal, he built on the work of Robert Greenleaf, adding the essential Christ-centered dimension.

Young has now taken this servant-leadership paradigm and put it at the heart of church renewal. He focuses here on three texts. First he takes us to Isaiah 40—55 and the Servant Songs of Isaiah, where he forces us to deal with ourselves as leaders and what we are to "be" before talking about church renewal and what we are to "do." In a key statement, he concludes, "Leadership for church renewal begins from the bottom up. It starts with learning to kneel, to listen to God, and to be attentive to directives from God" (28). From here, Young provides us with a compelling list of seven qualities, drawn from the Servant Songs of Isaiah. On these qualities he builds three movements of the Spirit, at the heart of renewing the leader for service: the upward, the inward, and the outward. Young maintains a consistent Christocentric methodology, never throwing us back upon ourselves to somehow conjure up renewal: "Servant leaders discover God in their midst and then point others toward God" (44). They see the Holy Spirit at work in and around them. They lead by undergoing personal renewal that enables them to discern the Spirit's movement and lead others in God's intended direction.

Young's second primary text is Revelation 7. He picks up the theme of the "Lamb that becomes the Shepherd and leads his people by springs of living water." Here he unpacks for us four dynamics of renewal: worship, transformation, the Lamb becoming the Shepherd (the model of servant leadership), and the Shepherd leading his people to renewal (living water).

In the Revelation text, Young has found an archetype of the servant leader in the Lamb of God and the Shepherd who leads. He expounds on this idea in chapter 4 by presenting four steps servant leaders need to take to prepare themselves for renewal. Again Young takes us first to the need for personal renewal before talking about the process of renewal for the church. In explaining these steps—listening to God, motivating the people, carrying the vision, and calling forth leaders—Young is as informative and inspiring as anywhere in the book. Every Christian leader will be blessed and challenged as they follow Young through this discussion.

Only after laying this foundation in personal transformation and spiritual renewal as leaders does Young finally direct us to the work of renewal in and for the church. Chapters 5, 6, and 7 are his handbook for church renewal, dealing with organizing for renewal, servant structures, and handling hardships. These chapters are rich with examples and lessons learned through his long history of leading and teaching church renewal.

Finally, Young takes us to John 13 and the humble event of Jesus washing of the feet of his disciples. In this "drama," Young finds both service and leadership that bring about and flow from the transforming work of the Holy Spirit. Through personal stories and biblical insights, Young ties together the themes he has been developing. In his conclusion, he seeks to bring us to our knees in humble service and to our feet for inspired leadership. The central theme is water—simple water that washes feet and spiritual water that brings refreshment and renewal.

Through the use of these three texts, Young's book breathes new life into the terms *servant leader, renewal,* and *transformation,* reclaiming them for the church's use. In doing so, this book may help inspire a new generation of transformational leaders through whom God can bring about Spirit-led renewal.

I expect that Young's work will be used widely for pastoral continuing education and as a seminary text. In both of these settings, it will be a most-welcome publication. We are continually searching for texts for our students that combine ministry experience with biblical and theological insight and coherence. We also need texts that are methodologically sound and genuinely inspirational, texts that can speak to our seasoned pastors and our beginning theological students. In *Servant Leadership for Church Renewal,* we have been given a gem.

I commend this book to you, and I am deeply grateful to David Young for this compelling contribution to the future of the church of Jesus Christ.

—*Scott Rodin, President*
Eastern Baptist Seminary
Wynnewood, Pennsylvania

Preface

This is a book on leadership written from the front lines. I didn't plan it that way. I had been a pastor for some years. Then, while giving spiritual care in a hospice program for the terminally ill, I began to teach and write out of those learnings. Eventually I was called back into the local church. There I had to reapply what I had taught—and I was glad to find that my writing seemed to be on target. This is a book on leadership by the church for the church.

In my doctor of ministry program, done during my first pastorate, I learned that a special kind of leadership fits church renewal: *a servant-leadership style* rooted in the Scriptures. From my study of the Gospel of John, I gleaned five marks of ministry. These became standard-bearers for practicing ministries that embody wholeness in Christ. The role of the servant stood out in this effort.[1]

As a young pastor just out of seminary, I became aware of the need for leadership training in the church. The laity often seemed to lack tools and knowledge to be effective when called into positions of leadership. They wanted to know how to proceed when chosen to lead. This was especially true as the local church became renewed and as members took on new leadership roles.

When I began to teach church renewal courses in the seminary, I saw the same need among leaders, lay and ordained, for guidance and practical resources. I also found that leaders needed an approach combining an emphasis on spiritual development with the practical labors of planning and organizing. This is what the servant leadership model offers.

This book is about the way to develop servant leadership in the church. We will plumb the Scriptures to understand the call to servant leadership. Then we will look specifically at practical matters of leadership in the congregation, regardless of the size or setting, as it relates to renewal. Pastors, church leaders, and church executives can use this book in a variety of ways: for developing a plan of ongoing renewal in the church, for interim pastorates, and even for starting new churches.

In study of the servant concept, I came upon the work of Robert K. Greenleaf, who coined the term "servant-leadership." I acknowledge the broad scope of his ideas through his monographs. Greenleaf has defined servant leadership and stressed seeing things whole. His contributions have been most helpful in teaching church leaders how to formulate a plan of renewal for the local church.

While some would discard servanthood as being too weak or servile, we will actually see how this concept from the Scriptures is a strong model of leadership. The nation of Israel, the early church, and Jesus himself defined their ministries through servanthood. This was costly, to be sure. However, there is an authentic ring to being faithful to God even when it entails hardship.

At the request of my students, the spiritual component of church renewal was placed first in the seminary course. It is also fundamental to the ideas in this book. Clearly, growing in spiritual depth is what leads us in all our endeavors in leadership and church renewal. This resource shows the need for a spiritual focus in leadership and how training for leadership, in a servant style, is instrumental in renewing the church as a faith community. That spiritual thread is what runs throughout this book, as we look at the whole concept of the springs of living waters.

For the emerging work on servant leadership and church renewal, I thank the students at the Eastern Baptist Theological Seminary. This American Baptist seminary on the edge of Philadelphia relates to many denominations. Over the years, I have included a unit on servant leadership in the courses I taught on church renewal. Courses on church renewal were later offered at the satellite of Bethany Theological Seminary of the Church of the Brethren, at Eastern Mennonite Seminary, and at Princeton Theological Seminary.

Eventually, at the invitation of Dr. Eric Ohlmann, the dean at Eastern Seminary, a separate course emerged on servant leadership. I was aware of how much the motifs of servant leadership nurture the spiritual life of both the leaders and the congregation. In the process, leaders and congregation take part in a dynamic transformation that is at the heart of the Christian life. Similar to the church renewal classes, students in a servant-leadership course formulated a leadership project for renewal, to be implemented in their local context of ministry.

I thank students in the church renewal and leadership courses for their enthusiastic response and input, which greatly aided this project. I especially thank Scott Rodin, president of Eastern Seminary, for his tremendous interest in transformational leadership and for the foreword.

I give credit to Glenn Koch at Eastern Seminary for his helpful work on the word *springs*, which became central imagery in this book. I also thank those persons who helped directly with this project: Richard Sisco read early drafts, and his encouragement kept the project moving. Kathleen Hayes, managing editor of the devotional periodical *The Secret Place*, helped straighten out the text.

I thank the kind persons of the Daylesford Abbey, who opened doors of hospitality and let me use their library for reflection and writing. I felt a kinship between my own tradition and the Norbertines. These pages reflect the ongoing prayer life of this community.

I thank the participants; the cosponsor, The Robert K. Greenleaf Center for Servant-Leadership;[2] and the many denominations that were supporting sponsors for the conference entitled "Servants of the Living Springs." Some of the materials in this book were presented in preliminary fashion there. That day helped confirm the servant-leader movement represented in these pages.

Appreciation for interviews goes to Heifer Project International and to members of the staff at their ranch, the International Livestock and Learning Center, Perryville, Arkansas. Frankie Reynolds, David Gill, Ken Herron, and Jack Rorex as well as others granted interviews or helpful dialogue. As a serving structure, their reflection greatly aided the chapter on servant leaders and servant structures.

I thank David Garber, book editor at Herald Press, and all the support staff, for the fine way they have worked with this book. I also thank the designer, Jim Butti, who captured the theme of the book so well on the cover.

One other important team always provides excellent help—my family. When entering an establishment, both my sons, Jonathan and Andrew, ask who the manager is. In play, Andrew often becomes the manager. So leadership and its manner has always been a great interest for them.

My wife, Joan, has been constantly supportive, has offered input, and has read numerous drafts. Her focus on keeping it practical has been a real help for readers. Her spirit is reflected in these pages. Indeed, this work expresses a lifelong focus on teamwork that has been part of our family endeavors.

Finally, I want to express gratitude to the One who leads us all. In the preparation of this manuscript, God's leading presence was quite real. The quiet waiting upon God's Spirit has guided and bolstered this project from the beginning to the joyous ending. The presence of Christ has guided and sustained. With Paul, I say, "Thanks be to God for his inexpressible gift!" (2 Cor. 9:15).

—*David S. Young*

Introduction

At the twenty-fifth anniversary celebration of our seminary class, Dr. Murray Wagner, Professor of Historical Studies at Bethany Theological Seminary, told us a story I will never forget.

One year Murray traveled to the Welsh Mountains during lambing season and observed English sheepdogs. The Welsh shepherds use these sheepdogs to keep the sheep in the fold, to gather in a stray, and to round up the sheep at night. The dogs keep the sheep moving by biting at their heels. They know how to snap and hiss. The dogs know what they want the sheep to do, and they bring it about in their own forceful way. English sheepdogs are trained to get the job done.

However, if the shepherd sics his dogs on the sheep too much, this harsh manner of handling them can degrade the market value of the sheep.[3] The evidence can be seen in their weight loss and shabby appearance. English sheepdogs are one-owner dogs, relating only to the shepherd who is their master. Murray soon learned to keep his distance from these dogs.

There are two other breeds of sheepdogs: the Great Pyrenees, and the Catalan Herder. They treat the sheep differently. They are much gentler, yet they get the same job done. These sheepdogs are actually reared with the lambs and thus bond with them. In a way, they think they are sheep. These dogs recognize that they have the same needs as the sheep, such as the need for water.

What differentiates these dogs from the sheep is that when the shepherd calls, the dogs respond. They are loyal and sensitive to the shepherd and are at one with his purposes. They eagerly listen to and obey the shepherd. While they are bonded to the sheep, the Great Pyrenees and the Catalan Herders can gently lead them and gather them into the fold. How different from the tactics of the sheepdogs in Wales![4]

While at first sight, types of sheepdogs may seem to have little in common with church leaders, we can certainly see some similarities. Certain leaders think they know what is best for people—and tell them so by their very manner. Other leaders identify with their people, have a shared vision, and work with them toward common goals. The sheep, the flocks whom Jesus the Shepherd loves and leads, are clearly better off under the care of leaders who are like the gentle Great Pyrenees or Catalan Herder sheepdogs rather than like the English sheepdogs.

Although some leaders may appear to be getting the job done, in the end the results in followers' lives will reveal the nature of the leadership under which they have been raised. I firmly believe that the best church leaders are gentle shepherds like the Good Shepherd, Jesus. They identify with their sheep. They become attuned to the presence of Jesus Christ and follow his lead. As the Scriptures reveal, we are all called to be servants of Christ and to take on his manner (Phil. 2:5-11). This makes a tremendous impact on the way a leader guides the people.

As we explore servant-style leading, we will look at our basic understanding of leadership. We seek to develop a biblical leadership model that implements and reflects our faith in the Good Shepherd. In a vacuum of leadership or when leadership panics, tactics of fear and intimidation can be used to "round up the flock." Our style of shepherding directly impacts the results, whether in approaching one who has strayed from the fold or in handling a touchy issue at a board meeting. Our leadership style will be evident to the flock, and the flock will respond accordingly.

People—like sheep—do better when handled gently and with respect. This builds rapport. The strength of the servant-leadership model is to labor as co-workers in ministry with the flock, called together by Christ. Trainers of sheepdogs in the Pyrenees supply a valuable key for fostering servant leadership in the church.

Servants know what nourishes people spiritually. Both sheepdogs and their sheep need water to survive in the mountains. Likewise, servant leaders must partake of what the Shepherd has called "living water" (John 4:7-15). These living waters are also called "springs" or "fountains" because they bubble up to everlasting life.

Servant leaders have clear spiritual tasks: to listen to Jesus the Shepherd and to help guide their flocks to those refreshing springs of living water. I call servant leaders "Shepherds by the Living Springs," for they both partake and lead others to the Living Springs that refresh and heal, that give abundant and eternal life.

As I wrote this book, I became more and more aware of the importance of this imagery of water in the Scriptures. Water often emerges to signify the life-giving presence of God and of the living Christ. Springs are not the stale waters of a cistern but are moving, active, fresh waters, bubbling up to give life. Water images the living Christ at work in our hearts. At the fountains of living water, transformation occurs. New life springs forth.

It is crucial that all leaders who want to drink of this water and lead others to it be attuned to the voice of the Shepherd of us all. For this to occur, leaders need to be refreshed at the same springs where everyone else drinks. From those waters, each leader emerges refreshed, with unique ministries to offer the church.

In the Christian community, each person is a valued member and may discover some unexpected gifts of leadership. Leadership roles may change. What becomes most important is responding to the chief Shepherd, Jesus Christ.

With this beautiful imagery in mind, church leaders can begin to sense God's love through their ongoing spiritual disciplines.[5] As they treat others with gentle compassion and care, their approach to leadership changes—and so does what happens in their churches. I have been struck time and again at how this change in the understanding of leadership makes all the difference in the world in church renewal. Church leaders can have a whole new energy and sense of hope. In the following pages, we will explore this in depth.

Many years ago, I was serving with the Bush Creek Church of the Brethren, in Monrovia, Maryland, outside Washington, D.C. While I worked at my task of implementing a plan for church renewal, this image of the servant leader emerged. As we grew as a congregation, I became aware of the many resources of both established members and new people. These people had a lot to offer!

However, most people need to be trained and nurtured for good servant leadership to occur in the church. Members need models and deliberate training to function in this manner. They need support for this kind of leadership to develop in the church.

We need to look at how such leadership is carried out both in specific tasks and in the overall development of the church. How do we create servant-style structures within a church community? How can we build a sense of teamwork between leaders and laity? How should differences of opinion and approach be handled?

I believe the Bible offers some clear guidance on servant leadership. In this book we will explore in depth several Scripture passages that point to the character of servant leadership and its application.

Transformation in faith is at the heart of Jesus' style of service, first observed in prayer and then in action with people. The dynamics for a servant-leader style of renewal spring forth from the biblical texts.

We will explore a whole range of topics that point to how servant leadership, spiritually rooted, can impact our work and renew the church. In the final pages of this book, we will draw together the images of water and see how we are "Shepherds by the Living Springs." This is an exciting journey.

The Lamb in the midst of the throne
will be their shepherd,
and he will guide them
to springs of living water.

—Revelation 7:17

1
A Vision for Leadership

Calvary Baptist Church is situated in the heart of Chester, Pennsylvania. That inner-city section is one of the five most blighted in the country. The threat of violence, fires, and drugs is all around. Nothing new seemed to be happening at Calvary Baptist—except that church members who could move away were doing so.

In the neighborhood around the church, more and more windows were being boarded up. All Pastor Tommy Jackson could do was keep inviting Sunday morning worshipers to move forward, to keep the dwindling group together in the large meeting room.

Like many other congregations, Calvary was in decline. It lost its previous pastor rather quickly. Like many parishes, it stood in the shadow of better days. Great Baptist leaders, including Martin Luther King Jr., had graced its pulpit. But in recent years, the regional economy has given out. Mustangs are no longer built at the nearby Ford plant, aluminum foil is not made at Reynolds, and ships are not launched from the shipyards.

However, Tommy Jackson was not willing to give up. He believed God had more in store for the congregation and for himself. That's when he enrolled in a church renewal class at Eastern Baptist Theological Seminary. Tommy believed that he needed to take stock of his idea of leadership before he could, with God's help, begin to turn his church around. He would dedicate himself to a more intentional time of Bible study and prayer.

Rather than carrying the load himself, Tommy felt that he needed to find what resources were available to him. He wanted to discover a leadership style that would begin with his faith and then encompass the needs so apparent on every side. He began by dedicating himself to a more intentional time of daily Bible study and prayer.

Six years later, Tommy speaks of a Calvary where people are "hanging from the balconies" and where a food pantry and homeless shelter serve those in need. On Saturday mornings, Chester residents gather at Calvary for a time of morning prayer and Bible study. Renovations are being made to the stately old church, including new pews and much-needed repainting.

The changes at Calvary began as Tommy did the daily class assignments. He began developing a deeper spiritual life of devotion and prayer. Tommy identified a biblical vision to guide him. He took to heart the advice of Jethro to Moses in Exodus 18: "Moses, you are carrying too heavy a load. Divide up your responsibilities." Tommy spoke in class about what he called "the lower road" in leadership, taking on the role of the servant. He learned how to divide his responsibilities among others and give up some control.

Tommy even did the unthinkable: in his planning, he divided the city of Chester into zones and assigned a deacon to each zone. Instead of the pastor being directly responsible for caring for each member, deacons would tend to the needs of the members in their zones, in a servant-leader style. If a new person appeared in church one Sunday, a deacon would make a follow-up call or visit. If someone was missing for several Sundays, the deacon would make a call. In fact, every member would receive a routine contact each quarter.

In church-renewal language, Tommy developed what could be called a "plan for ministry." He asked the crucial question for any church: How will we as a congregation take our vision and translate it into practical reality? Calvary members didn't take some master plan borrowed from another congregation. Their plan of ministry was tailored to their own congregation. Calvary discovered that with its leadership so oriented and its members on board, ministry happened naturally and intentionally. It didn't need special techniques or gimmicks. As a result, the congregation stabilized and then grew about 35 percent.

At the end of the first three-year phase of the intentional plan of renewal, Tommy felt a new focus was needed. Rather than just relying on the deacons to respond to needs, he decided to hold a training institute on servant leadership, for the whole congregation. Tommy found a new Scripture for this thrust, this time from Revelation, and he worked on building each person's potential. He developed sessions on servant leadership, to which all members were invited.

Using various Scriptures on the inner life of the leader, Tommy helped them identify and improve their leadership potential. They looked at qualities essential to leadership and how to develop effective leadership skills. The outcomes are spreading as a new plan is implemented. Attendance has grown 100 percent.

Leadership and Servanthood

Where can the church find good models for leadership in our modern society? We can certainly find some good in various management theories. But in times of personal and medical crisis, often the world looks to the church and to spiritual leaders for help. The spiritual dimension, emerging in many management theories, is recognized as essential for fulfillment. How many people and families long for a touch of spiritual healing! When a culture is searching for moorings and values and spiritual depth, it naturally turns to the church to provide some form of leadership.

To point others toward new life and faith, we need to develop a vision for leadership that helps us go deeper in faith and puts our faith and vision into practice. Such reflection draws us toward developing a concept of leadership that begins with our faith. We need to listen to God and to be rooted in the experiences of God's people, as shown in Scripture. Our vision for leadership then extends to all we do in the church and to all the situations to which we relate, as the church in the world.

From Scripture, a leadership model emerges. In the Scriptures we have major examples of leadership to guide us. Prophets, priests, sages, and kings were all leaders. Each of these types had a clear role or calling.

Prophets called the people to the covenant and to faithfulness. They were voices for the Lord, urging the people to turn back to God (Jer. 1–2; Isa. 6).

Leadership was also expressed through priests. They had a mission to help Israel know God's law and be "a light to the nations" (Isa. 49:6; Mal. 2:7; 2 Chron. 15:3; Exod. 19:6).

Sages shared wise counsel to help their people deal with daily life in "the fear of the Lord" (Prov. 1:7).

Finally, there was the king, a borrowed leader type. Samuel reminded the people that the Lord was already their king. But the people wanted to have rulers "like other nations." A king was chosen and anointed to be a central symbol, a leading representative of the people before God. He was accountable to God for carrying out duties of kingship, working for justice, and protecting the weak (1 Samuel 8, 10; Ps. 72).

Each of these leadership roles found a useful place in Israel. Yet each leader type turned inward upon itself.

Rather than pointing people to their faith covenant with God, prophets began to degenerate into a professional trade, serving nationalism rather than the call of God (1 Kings 22).[6] They enticed the people to follow other gods (Deut. 13, 18; Jer. 23).

Instead of mediating the covenant and leading the people to obey God, priests began to define holiness as following prescribed rituals. That only inflated their own importance and distracted the people from doing justice (Ps. 50:8-13; Amos 5:21-25; 7:10-13).

The sages sometimes might have discouraged people by giving grim and almost hopeless pictures of life. "Vanity of vanities! All is vanity" (Eccles. 1:2; 9:1-6; 12:8). Rather than representing the people before God and coming to the aid of the needy, kings reveled in their power. They reigned at the expense of other people and made alliances with other nations that were not God-centered (1 Kings 3:1; 11:1-13). In each case, leadership lost its vision, staying power, and strength.

Emerging through all these fallen traditions, however, is the model of the servant, who comes to play a key leadership role. For example, the prophet Jeremiah saw himself as a lad, literally meaning a servant (Jer. 1:6). Priests were supposed to help the people see that they had a mission to perform to the nations. Finally, the prime task of kings was defined in terms of service, to take care of the poor and widow.

Actually, after the defeat of the nation, servanthood in its clearest form is delineated by a special prophet, Isaiah. As we see later, the servant role is most fully fleshed out in Jesus, especially as God's anointed one takes up the basin and towel.

In Isaiah 40–55, an author some refer to as "Second Isaiah" clearly describes the servant role. Central to his writings are four so-called Servant Songs, expressing the characteristics of the servant: Isaiah 42:1-4; 49:1-6; 50:4-11; 52:13—53:12. You may wish to refer to these passages now. They are crucial to the discussion of servants and servant leaders.

We need to plumb the Scriptures and look ever more deeply into the center of our own spiritual lives and into the lives of people in the church. In so doing, we can develop our unique biblical vision for leadership within our own church. Such a vision can capture the best of our imaginations, the best of our talents, and the best of our energies. In leadership, we meet all of the temptations earlier leaders did. Yet in leading as servants, we grow in faith. Leadership is not only doing things but also modeling our faith in our very being. Servants become leaders. Such a vision for servant leadership has direct implications for vitality in the church. Being a leader of church renewal begins with servanthood.

For so many years, in approaching the church we have used a diagnostic model of renewal: Find out what's wrong and fix it. With such a model, we tend to project large dreams that often are unrealized. Expectations built up are often unrealistic and even sometimes unfaithful to God. Christian theologian Dietrich Bonhoeffer spoke of how God helps us get rid of such false wish dreams. That is essential for true community to emerge.[7]

Leadership for church renewal begins by focusing on our sense of God's leading. We discern our God-given vision, find out what's going right in our particular church, and build on it. When we identify what's going right, that is usually the key to God-given talents in this unique mission of God. Each church has its own key role in the kingdom. Each church has a path of renewal and vitality for its own situation, which may differ from other congregations. By affirming strengths within the local church, good leaders can point the way.

Leadership for church renewal begins from the bottom up. It starts with learning to kneel, to listen to God, and to be attentive to directives from God. Godly leaders recognize their need to drink from the waters of the Living Springs just like everyone else does. Kneeling also means serving the needs of others and lifting them up in affirmation. Rather than superimposing their ideas on everyone else, servant leaders call forth the gifts of others.

Embodying servant-style leadership means recognizing

just how important it is to keep attuned to the Good Shepherd and at critical times to know how to point the way for others. By being in fellowship with others who have been called into service, leaders can help guide and support them. Servanthood is what guides us in thinking about leadership and church renewal.

In establishing a biblical approach to leadership, we see how the term *servant* exemplifies what leadership in the church is all about. Robert Greenleaf says it so well: "The servant-leader *is* servant first. . . . It begins with the natural feeling that one wants to serve, to serve *first*. Then conscious choice brings one to aspire to lead."[8] This approach arises out of examining the biblical model of servanthood. We see how one feels led to serve God, and out of that motivation, to serve others. From there, true renewal can begin for the church.

Leadership therefore is a spiritual work, attuning oneself to the Shepherd and following the lead of God's Spirit as exemplified in Jesus Christ. Rather than some magical management theory, this style of leadership is rooted in faithfulness to God and in spiritual growth. With an ear to the Shepherd and to the needs of others, servant leaders can hear the call for a new vision of leadership in the church, a vision that points to renewal and enlists fellow servants.

Rather than working themselves out of a job, servant leaders help others to become servants and thus also servant leaders. Thus the church becomes a serving community with all the marks and manner of Christ.

To fully understand what servant leadership means for church renewal, we must first define the servant and the servant leader—those who are most fit to lead a congregation in its spiritual journey. Out of such a vision, we will see how a process can emerge for renewal of the church. In all this, God provides the very life of life. So we will return again and again to the theme that we are shepherds by the Living Springs.

The Servant of Second Isaiah

The nation of Israel (at least the upper level of its society) was living in exile in Babylonia during a time of loss and hardship, in what we call the second captivity. This happened because the people disobeyed God and their kings made political alliances with countries that did not know the Lord.

Just when all seems lost and the people are feeling in disfavor with God, Second Isaiah speaks out. He announces God's grace and extends a call to Israel to become a new community with a renewed mission as servants. God calls them to be a servant people.

Without moving far from the topic of church renewal, we will certainly see parallels as we explore what this author means by servanthood. In the narrative of Scripture, we can sense the reality in our situation and identify with the biblical story. This is our story. Whenever a congregation or denomination discovers it has lost its vitality, despair and self-doubt can set in. Everyone can feel discouraged. A lack of focus is apparent. Spirit is lost.

Through servanthood, God's people can find an entirely new role, to be servants of God. Behind this movement of servanthood in the biblical account is the emergence of priestly writers who see new life tied to creation itself. For the priestly writers, who are active in the exile, everything is dependent for its existence upon the sovereign God (Isa. 40).[9] God calls life into being. Creation sets the stage for history.

When Israel is in the depths of desolation, the priestly writers hold up hope in new life that comes from God. For them, such new vitality is discovered by staying close to God in worship that is reflected in life so centered in God as to find new wholeness and hope.[10]

In that unique context, a writer known as Second Isaiah emerges whose words about the Servant echo through

Isaiah 40–55. The refrains in his book, which include the four unique Servant Songs, are so elegantly expressed that they are repeatedly used in the New Testament. Later they are transcribed by Handel in the oratorio *Messiah*.

In the synagogue at Nazareth, Jesus himself quotes from one of the refrains in Isaiah 61:1-2, thought by some to be part of Second Isaiah, to inaugurate his own ministry:

> The Spirit of the Lord is upon me,
>   because he has chosen me
>   to bring good news to the poor.
> He has sent me to proclaim liberty to the captives
>   and recovery of sight to the blind,
> to set free the oppressed
>   and announce that the time has come
>   when the Lord will save his people.
>   (Luke 4:18-19, GNB)

What a message with a vision for a mission! Used by Jesus to define his own purpose, we see how such a vision emerged in a time of new focus.

Unusual as it may seem at first, the biblical promise is that God's people will be transformed from servitude to servanthood. Israel's new clarity about its calling is coupled with a new world consciousness. Ordinarily one expects that in defeat people would turn inward and work at self-preservation. That would certainly be tempting. Is it not disgraceful to be so plundered? They might well wonder how they could be used for anything in this situation.

Nevertheless, Second Isaiah sees God's activity otherwise—as One extending grace. He calls out, " 'Comfort my people,' says our God. 'Comfort them!' " (Isa. 40:1, GNB) When all seems gloom and doom, this herald has good news. The prophet projects expectancy and hope. Here is a vision and model for refocusing one's purpose, a model for renewal of mission. This is the "dawn of a new era." [11]

In a similar way, a congregation can experience a shift as it finds a new vision. Congregations can be released from forces that bind and restrict them: loss of motivation, laborious meetings, and troubling budgets. All of these direct energies inward and indicate some deeper need.

A new focus with a clear vision can redirect energies that otherwise only maintain the status quo. A new vision provides a much-needed focus that people can affirm. Servants see that these "same old people" can do something new and can be used by God. Servants are those who can see such new possibilities.

Who is this Servant in Isaiah? A particular person, or a nation? At one and the same time, the Servant seems to be an individual and a body of people. At times the Servant personifies the people's deepest call. Collected in its meanings is the idea of the one and the many, an individual representing the group and the group representing the individual.

In any case, the idea is quite revolutionary. God's favor has always been associated with power over others, with conquest and victory. Now God's call is envisioned as working in a redemptive manner as the Servant. Each person is part of this mission!

Servants are therefore called by God at a unique time in the history of humankind. They provide the leadership to focus the world again on God's movement and presence. Being a servant is usually not a popular role. It involves lowly work in meeting others' needs. Yet servants grow into unique and godly human beings. Servants provide a leadership style that is powerful in an unexpected way. Servants point people to God's vision for them.

Servants and Servant Leaders

The best leaders are servants—servants of God and servants of the people. To be a leader, one must first be a servant. What characterizes servants and servant leaders? Seven qualities emerge biblically in the Servant Songs in Second Isaiah.

First, servant leaders feel *a sense of calling*, a calling to serve God. God has a purpose for them to fulfill: to mediate covenant and bring others into God's will. They do this through becoming servants. This is what defines them, informs them, and guides them. In other words, servant leaders serve.

In response to God's grace, such persons serve God, and in so doing, they serve people out of gratitude. They begin to reflect the presence of God and carry the message of God in their hearts, reflecting it in and through their very being. This is evident right from the start of Second Isaiah: "Speak tenderly to Jerusalem, and cry to her that her warfare is ended, that her iniquity is pardoned" (Isa. 40:2).

With this call, the Servant is assured that God will provide the strength for the task. God's Spirit is with the Servant. So the first Servant Song begins, "The Lord says, 'Here is my servant, whom I strengthen'" (Isa. 42:1, GNB). Even though there will be tough times as this Servant becomes a leader, God will continue to provide strength and not let the Servant falter.

The second trait of the servant leader is seen in the personal and *humble manner*. The Servant experiences internal change to humility and does not cry aloud in public, making a big scene. The Servant leader carries the truth in the same humble way it was received. Rather than overpowering those already weakened, the Servant leader works in a humble manner. "A bruised reed he will not break, and a dimly burning wick he will not quench" (Isa. 42:3). There is gentleness in this Servant's manner.

Third, servant leaders lead from *a heart of peace*. This is evident from their very mode and manner. So much of leadership is connecting with what is happening within people, discerning gifts, and connecting people in ministry. This trait can be costly, leading to self-sacrifice. The Servant is a suffering Servant (as in Isaiah 53) because self-emptying before God is crucial to the very meaning of serving. Servants learn the path of forgiveness, of obedience, of self-sacrifice. This is not an easy path. Rather than seeking fame and fortune, servant leaders learn the satisfaction of being faithful to their calling, even when it is small and humble.

Fourth, the servant leader has *a clear vision*. All through the Servant Songs in Second Isaiah, we see the tremendous vision of one called by God for a purpose, to establish justice and a right-ordered society. In Isaiah 49, the Servant is called from birth and in every part of personal existence to gather Israel back to God. "Before I was born, the Lord appointed me; he made me his servant to bring back his people" (49:5, GNB).

Second Isaiah calls the people to be a light to the nations (49:6). Their purpose is to extend that vision of the Lord's salvation for all humanity. Servants hold this vision to the fore and help others join in teamwork effort to fulfill their mission. Such a vision becomes an integral part of who one really is called to be in this unique time and place for God. Servant leaders fulfill a mission both for themselves and for others.

Because of their unique style, servant leaders point the way. Rather than simply reacting to crises or being unfaithful to their values, they are steadfast in following their vision. Servant leaders have the unique ability to see things whole, like Matthew Arnold's friend "who saw life steadily and saw it whole." They see how this vision can be implemented; they have a unique ability to see how things can fit together. They reflect a godly creativity.

Fifth, the Servant also *listens*. In the third song, the Lord actually opens the servant's ear every morning. Servanthood originates with attentiveness to God. "Morning by morning he wakens—wakens my ear to listen as those who are taught." (Isa. 50:4b, NRSV). This song ties such listening with obedience, staying close to God. Listening to God's leadings sets the direction for servant leaders. First they listen to God, and from what they hear, they develop a sense of how God is leading them to meet the needs of those about them. Like prophets, servant leaders call others to open their ears to the Lord, to allow their ears to be opened by God, so they will have godly sensitivity in the words they themselves speak.[12] Being so taught and so obedient means the servant is a disciple.

It may seem paradoxical to so emphasize the role of listening because we often think of leaders as people who do a lot of talking! Robert Greenleaf speaks poignantly about the role of listening: "Only a natural servant automatically responds to any problem by listening *first*. When he is a leader, this disposition causes him to be seen as servant first."[13]

In a real sense, listening deepens levels of communication and understanding. Listening has a way of strengthening others, helping them clarify who they are and how they might grow. We will talk more about listening, as it is a practical tool for servant leaders in finding a vision for a renewal plan.

Sixth, a paradoxical trait is that the Servant does not have a dazzling appearance. Usually one associates beauty with success. However, according to Second Isaiah, a Servant leader doesn't dress for success or develop a spectacular personality or physique. Instead, the Servant has a heart of suffering for others.

The Servant is chosen for good *inner qualities* rather than outward appearance: "He had no form or majesty that we should look at him, nothing in his appearance that we should desire him" (Isa. 53:2, NRSV). "The Lord looks on the heart" (1 Sam. 16:7) and uses the Servant to accomplish the purpose and vision set forth.

As we move into church renewal, we may begin to feel

that we aren't cut out for it. Some of us can hardly imagine ourselves serving in a soup kitchen. We think we don't have what it takes to be a teacher or a first-class administrator in the office.

Besides, how is old First Church ever going to have the stuff to make a significant ministry happen? We don't have those kinds of people here! That's for others who have more money, more education, or more whatever.

Nevertheless, God's servants are those who know their limitations but begin to realize that God can use even them.

Seventh, the last trait builds on all the others: In apparent weakness, the power of God is revealed. The servant leader experiences *power in weakness* (cf. 2 Cor. 12:9; 4:7). Even those delivered are astonished that it is the Servant who inaugurates their release. Therein they recognize the role and importance of the Servant.

In Israelite history, serving meant to be in disfavor with God, especially when it was combined with suffering. Now the Servant through suffering obtains life, and by that role leads others into finding reconciliation with God. Servants and servant leaders receive life and honor: "The will of the Lord shall prosper in his hand" (Isa. 53:10).

Servants and servant leaders who want to help churches be renewed need to be open to an element of surprise. Some may say, "While we wished it could happen, we never thought it was possible." They have a sense of disbelief, of serendipity. It is not through their own power, schedule, and plans that renewal happens. This is why there is a song on their hearts. Servants feel an inner sense of being lifted up and led by God.

These four passages of Second Isaiah express beyond words what a true Servant is. People who are willing servants are key in deliverance and renewal because they lift the spirits of others as they open themselves to God. They mediate the covenant of God through their very presence. In a real sense, servants carry a song of God's deliverance in their hearts. Thus our vision for renewal begins. Thus our mission is defined.

The Lift of the Servant Leader

Servant leaders have a special lift. That is because of what they have in their hearts—a unique sense of a call from God to serve. Perhaps it is the story of the sheepdogs that best illustrates it. While bonded with the sheep, they hear the voice of the shepherd and serve the needs of those who are around them. All the traits of the Servant are part of who they are.

Finally, servant leaders are sustained by a song, a unique spirit in their hearts that is transmitted to others. This is what spells joy for them in their labors, which are certainly taxing at times. They feel the lift that the writer of Second Isaiah felt and expressed in chapter 55, at the close of this section in the book:

> *For you shall go out in joy,*
> *and be led back in peace;*
> *the mountains and the hills before you*
> *shall burst into song,*
> *and all the trees of the field shall clap their hands.*
> (Isa. 55:12, NRSV)

2
Leading for Spiritual Growth

Putting Christ at the heart of all renewal projects is crucial. Being Christ-centered means that all our efforts originate from and focus on Jesus Christ. From Christ comes both power and grace. In him we experience the hope that is at the heart of new life and wholeness. The very paradox of redemption is that in surrender and obedience, God gives life. Servant leaders keep their eyes and ears centered on Jesus.

Early in my teaching career, students requested that I place the spiritual component first in my courses. As I did, references to the spiritual dimension started to become more and more a part of what I presented. I discovered that servant leadership is all about the spiritual, tapping the resources of God's Spirit. Servant leaders listen to God and discern the movements of spiritual life within themselves and within the church.

Renewal therefore is never just a program one can design and implement. We might think that if we develop just the right program and have just the right people, everything will fall into place. But true renewal is never just a committee and its work. Renewal is freeing the congregation from whatever is binding it so that all participants can fully use their gifts in ministry.

Renewal occurs as a congregation discovers the love of Christ, which gathers the church as a shepherd does the lambs. As we move into dynamics of renewal, we discover how being "in Christ" takes on a central meaning in renewal.

Spiritual Movements and the Path of Renewal

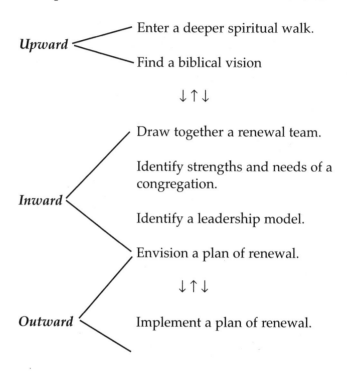

Upward — Enter a deeper spiritual walk.
— Find a biblical vision

↓ ↑ ↓

Inward — Draw together a renewal team.

Identify strengths and needs of a congregation.

Identify a leadership model.

Envision a plan of renewal.

↓ ↑ ↓

Outward — Implement a plan of renewal.

Rather than enslaving us, coming into obedience to Christ is life-giving through servanthood. That shift comes as one understands one's call, purpose, and ministry. The word *ministry* comes from the root word "servanthood." Being "in Christ" takes on special meaning in the New Testament. There is a call to fidelity to Christ on one hand, and the experience of Christ's sheltering presence on the other. Such rootedness in Christ is needed for any church that would find a vision in a world that is secular, needy, and often chaotic. "In Christ" spells freedom, direction, and joy.

As I formulated a sevenfold process of organizing for

renewal, I could actually picture three movements of spiritual growth. These movements infiltrated the organizational elements of shaping a plan of ministry. In this chapter we look at the three movements of spiritual vitality—upward, inward, and outward—and the sevenfold path of renewal they create. This is depicted in the chart.

Not to be forgotten in renewal is the real need for spiritual guidance, which is the task of leaders. These movements toward spiritual growth are crucial in planning and implementing a church renewal process.

One hot and humid day, I went to take a shower and found that the tub just kept filling and filling. No water would go down the drain. First I tried to remove any debris and then applied my plunger to the drain, with no success. So I paused to think for a moment. In that pause, I wondered, *Could it be, could it just be that the drain lever is up rather than down? No, that would be too simple an answer.* But with a flip, you guessed it, down went the water!

This story illustrates what can happen when we step back to reflect on our situation. In any difficult circumstance, the servant leader needs to listen to the Spirit. All too often, the spiritual call of pastors and other church leaders gets lost in the midst of keeping programs going, planning for Sunday mornings, dealing with crises and "closed drains," and handling everything else that needs to be done.

Being an effective spiritual leader means helping individuals become aware of opportunities for growth in their spiritual lives. It means helping them learn to live their lives as disciples called to love and serve Jesus. It means helping a congregation that is in bondage become aware of God's power in Christ and find release from that bondage. It means leading the congregation to be transformed by God's grace and attuned to its call to be a servant people. Spiritual growth involves pausing in front of obstacles to find the solution, the path to refreshment and renewal.

We can see three movements of spiritual growth. First

we point upward to God, receiving God's grace; then inward, to the transformation in God's love; and finally outward, to serve God and others. From servitude to servanthood—what a challenge! Let us look in greater detail at the three movements that together define the sevenfold path of renewal to be followed, as described in later chapters.

The Upward Call

The upward movement occurs when people become aware of God's grace and experience that grace extending to the church and each of its members. The songs of Second Isaiah, examined in chapter 1, can lead the people into an awareness of the freedom and grace of God. That grace can release them and restore them and sustain them as servants. Servant people have a daily awareness of God's Spirit and the Spirit's life-giving power.

In the Servant Songs (Isa. 42:1-4; 49:1-6; 50:4-11; 52:13—53:12), we see how God opens the ear of the Servant every day. Listening is more than our doing as servants. Morning by morning, God tugs at our ears (50:4). God takes the initiative. Servants develop a sense of God's loving presence drawing them to life-giving purposes.

In all the leadership and church renewal projects with which I have worked, pastors and church leaders began by becoming more intentional in their own spiritual pilgrimages. They were not necessarily spiritually dead. In fact, they were alive enough to feel some nudges from without or urges from within to become more open to God's movement.

They intentionally established disciplines of faith, needed for themselves and others to grow. They set up daily plans of Bible study, prayer, and quiet time. They began prayer journals or plotted out regular times for personal spiritual retreats (on deepening a spiritual walk, see worksheet 1, at the back of this book). Through these disciplines, individuals can become more aware of God's movement in their lives.

In response to the need for spiritual renewal, church members often establish prayer groups or what we will call a renewal team. Like the Servant in the songs of Second Isaiah who felt God's call, people begin to talk about the movement of God's Spirit that they have begun to feel. As a result, a church may decide to hold a prayer vigil or a spiritual retreat, where major personal renewal and spiritual growth can occur.

In growth through prayer, God's grace and love become more real in people's lives. God turns their hearts and faces upward. They discover a new movement of God's Spirit. Something more is possible. They do not need to stay in the former bondage; they find comfort and hope for what is to come.

The Elizabethtown Church of the Brethren, with which I worked as interim associate pastor, took this upward turn a few years ago. This is a college-town church, with 350 or more in attendance on an average Sunday. Many members of the congregation are formally educated, and the church has a multiple staff.

At its heart is a deep care for people. It has about three layers of leadership organization. Some committees or assignments are long-standing, some newer and younger, and some identified but still to be developed. As a church, Elizabethtown was eager for renewal, especially to develop ministries for younger and older members.

After hearing just one presentation on the process and the path to renewal, its envisioning committee decided to hold a special series of Lenten meetings on Sundays and Wednesdays. On Sunday mornings, sermon topics were from Ephesians. On Wednesday evenings, the congregation joined in singing and then listened to a message from the pastor, delving deeper into the text of the previous Sunday. This was followed by small group discussions. The envisioning committee also provided a kids' club for the children. Someone said that in the past, no one would come to such events. This time the response was outstanding. At first fifty people came; then seventy came to the series. The children's program drew over thirty. People began to share about their faith. The music lifted and encouraged us. Momentum grew. The small groups that met for discussion did not want to close. God's grace and God's love was becoming real.

As the series drew to a close, many persons expressed a desire to continue Wednesday evening services year-round. Moreover, our youth ministry, which was just starting to take hold, received a giant impetus to move forward. We launched a youth ministry advisory team and then a senior high youth program. The momentum from the spiritual journey upward to God in prayer, study, and sharing was real.

The secret to this kind of renewal lies in understanding the need for "living water" and learning to feed and nurture people in their faith (John 4:10-11; 7:38; Jer. 2:13; 17:13). The Christian leader must keep this as the church's central focus. So much of the daily work and maintenance of the church can seem mundane. Nevertheless, the servant leader sees how ordinary experiences are connected with the spiritual growth of the congregation and the daily ministry of God's people. This turns common interactions into ones that point to the living water, the fountains of life.

Jesus was a Master at such interactions. His life and teachings continually pointed people to what they were searching for in their lives. Where is God's grace becoming evident in your life and in the church? Step by step, we move toward more awareness of God's Spirit, God's grace, and the movements of God's Spirit. Every such step is central to renewal itself.

In other words, renewal in the church is ongoing. It is not something to be done once a year—or once and for all.

Spiritual renewal entails a constant process of becoming attuned to God's leadings. Servant leaders continually keep their eyes and ears attuned to the Good Shepherd. Here one finds the springs of living water running freely.

At the same time, servant leaders keep their eyes and ears on others. They respond to the needs that become apparent as they walk in faith. They point those who are thirsty to the springs of enrichment. Servant leaders discover God in their midst and then point others toward God. Servant leaders follow the lead of God's Spirit.

Through the spiritual disciplines in this movement upward, we will often feel drawn to some biblical passage that speaks God's message of grace and hope. As we will see in more detail in chapter 3, a vision for renewal and the very dynamics of renewal can often be revealed in a text to which we feel drawn. The biblical story of release from bondage can become our story. The great themes of deliverance, salvation, and resurrection can become ours.[14]

God's grace is revealed as we turn upward. In so doing, we recognize our need for help. As we listen to God's Spirit and experience God's grace reaching into our lives, we catch a vision that draws us ever into God's love.

The Inward Movement

On the heels of the first movement upward comes a second movement, inward. This movement involves a transformation of the heart that deepens the understanding of our spiritual call.

In a real sense, Israel moves from servitude to servanthood. Before the change, the Israelites were in servitude to pursuing their sense of power. Rather than remaining faithful to God, they gave their energy to figuring out how to outmaneuver others politically. They sought to come out on top, even at the expense of compromising their own faith and values. Eventually defeated, they saw no way out.

The Israelites felt cut off from their source of life and cut off from one another. Isolated, the people ask how they can worship in a foreign land (Ps. 137). Their inner transformation, envisioned by Isaiah and other prophets of the period, comes through the Shepherd who will gather the people into his loving arms (Isa. 40:11; Ezek. 34). For Isaiah, that transformation is total; the very deserts spring forth with life-giving waters. The people of God come to understand that they are a called-out people. God's love transforms— both individually and corporately.

In this second movement, inward, servant leaders become aware of such transformation in themselves and in the church. God controls this transformation in which people feel they are no longer just reacting to their situation. With God's help, they experience that transformation first within themselves and later within the church. In both cases, God's love and presence become more real.

Sometimes this inward change happens in the more-intentional time of worship and prayer, or through an intense study of a Scripture passage. Sometimes the change happens as a pastor forms a prayer pact with a prayer group, with the deacons, or with the entire congregation. Sometimes it happens when the congregation meets and identifies their strengths. It could happen elsewhere along the path of renewal.

Transformation happens as a new wholeness with God and others is felt. This shows some fulfillment of the "new covenant" (Jer. 31:31; 1 Cor. 11:25). Regardless of the time and place, people begin to experience hope, and they feel that their lives can be used by God.

In other words, transformation can never be just individual because renewal is not just individual. Renewal is both individual and corporate. I will never forget the response of one woman in a survey. When I asked whether she felt the growth in her church would continue, she replied, "I'm growing, and therefore I know we're growing." This is the sense of the servant—that at one and the same time, the servant is an individual and is part of the corporate body.

It is best for us to start the process of renewal by affirming a mutual covenant together and with God. We realize that this is a teamwork effort touching every person in the church. Each person's discoveries can be cherished, and each one builds up the others. Growth is experienced as a mutual endeavor. In a serving congregation, each member monitors what is happening in the whole church.

To facilitate such inward renewal, I suggest implementing four steps in the path of renewal (see worksheets 3-6): First, draw together a renewal team. Second, identify the strengths and needs of the congregation. Third, identify a leadership model. Fourth, envision a plan of renewal.

Let us review these steps briefly from the vantage of the servant leader.[15] Before one goes too far into the process, the servant leader in a congregation should first gather a team of people who can share in this exploration of inner renewal. Usually this is a combination of people in the structure of that church as well as other participants who want to explore renewal. This is a team effort; renewal can never be a solo project.

Teams model the church, call forth the gifts of individuals, and work in a Christ-centered way. It is important for the servant leader to share the key biblical text the leader has been working on. The team can work together on that text, if it feels appropriate, or it can select another text to supply some guiding imagery of renewal.

A second step is to identify the strengths and needs of a congregation. Often we use a diagnostic model for renewal: find out what is wrong and fix it. However, the strengths of a congregation can point us to where God-given talents are present and where spiritual nurture is happening. Renewal can begin by focusing on what is right rather than what is wrong.

An early project of the renewal team may be to hold a congregational event at which people share in small groups where their spiritual lives have been nurtured and where the strengths and needs of their church lie. From there, common themes often emerge to shape a vision for renewal. Inward transformation may occur as a congregation goes through this meaningful exercise. Often members feel empowered to claim their future.

The third step is to claim the servant-leadership model for renewal. In such a model, the leader is aware of serving in response to God's grace. Servant leaders serve Christ, and in serving Christ, they serve others, who also learn to serve through God's grace.

A workshop, or in-service training, may be held in the church to review the points of servant leadership: servants have a vision, act in a kindly manner, and lead from a heart of peace. Servants are able to listen deeply first to God and then to each other in discerning how renewal can occur. A renewal team can explore what servant leaders do and see how they serve a vision and serve our Lord.

Fourth, identify a theme of renewal and envision a plan. Envisioning involves moving from the inward to the outward. Seeing the biblical vision as well as the strengths and needs of a congregation, the team asks, "How can we as servants envision a plan of renewal? How can such a plan unfold naturally, step by step, over a three-year period? How can the dynamics of renewal from the biblical text enrich and guide such a plan?"

As they work, the team can diagram their plan on newsprint, showing how they would apply the biblical vision in a way that fits their specific congregation. This may take several drafts until they find one that is best.

Returning to our project at Elizabethtown, the envisioning committee identified youth ministry as the top priority for the congregation. At the same time, we saw how a youth ministry council would be formed.

A ministry to third, fourth, and fifth-graders was already being formed. They called themselves the Brethren Buddies. They already had well-received recreational events and were ready to add service projects.

The beginnings of a youth club for junior high was also underway. Their activities included recreation, meals, service projects, study times, and a choir.

The vision was to form a youth ministry council as a think tank. They would formulate mission, enlist advisers, arrange for training, and shape the work. They began by selecting a senior high youth cabinet that would be youth driven, with advisers to counsel. The cabinet would plan the program for senior high youths.

The council also began to look into how to strengthen the programming for young adults. They are becoming active in promoting training for the advisers and have been asked to cosponsor a training event on youth ministry at the local parish resource center.

An inward transformation is underway. The youths are developing their spiritual lives. People in the congregation are beginning to feel that they are getting a handle on a much-needed and much-desired ministry with youths.

The inward movement is part of the total transformation. People are changed. Churches are changed. As they move from despondency, there is hope. There is a future.

The Outward Path

This leads into a third movement of renewal: the movement outward, in which we discover grace and strength in serving. The writer of the Servant Songs certainly could identify with the pilgrimage of the people. As they discovered their role as servants, their faith and trust deepened. That shift comes as we understand our call, our purpose, and our ministry.

In serving, we meet our limits, test our patience, become

tired, and discover Christ. We learn about Jesus as we are down on the floorboards with him, washing feet. As we serve others, our faith deepens.

We see this third movement concretely as we envision and then implement a renewal plan. At this point, the real work of renewal is often overlooked. Here we are growing into our own ministry through practice. By serving and calling others into service, we are growing in grace. In the ups and downs, we experience the movement of Christ in both surrender and exultation. Implementing our renewal plan deepens our spiritual life. We grow as a serving body, becoming more Christlike and growing as a servant people.

As servant leaders at Elizabethtown implemented the youth ministry plan, the outward journey became clear. First we established organizational structures. Then with youths' suggestions, we called people to fill leadership roles. Most of these participants agreed to serve. The renewal team performed a vital ministry as it invited members with leadership gifts to help establish a youth ministry. A spiritual awareness grew that our faith can call someone to youth ministry, who then serves from thankfulness for grace received through the church.

Each of the groups is now involved in an outward movement: they are running their own programs and implementing their own service projects. At a crucial time for the junior high youths, when some inner tensions were brewing, they went to an inner-city church project. The inner-city youths in the most destitute of situations shared with our youth group. Many of the inner-city youths had been turned around from lives of drugs.

Our youths served in helping with a day camp for children on the streets. They took toys for a health clinic and food for church members. Our youths were touched by the faith of these people. In the process, they put their own conflicts behind them and grew stronger. A bond has grown, and they want to share it with others.

Finally, service has developed through singing, the traditional way the youth club has served the church. But they have gone far beyond the usual. The junior high youths led an entire worship service, complete with a spacecraft that descended by wire from the sanctuary balcony to the front of the chancel. Out of it, by some stratagem, the youths emerged. They shared about the meaning of "church" and concluded with an original upbeat composition by the music director (see facing page).

As we are stretched to our limit by reaching outward, we find we must depend on God to provide. The promise of Second Isaiah in 49:1-6 is that Servants will be honored and given strength even when they feel their labor has been in vain (cf. 40:31). Servants are lights to the nations. As we are stretched to the limit, we find we depend on God to provide.

One can tell a church being renewed by its outreach. When a church is touching lives, caring for others, and inviting them into a relationship with the living Lord, it is in renewal. Its servants are sharing the Living Springs with others in word and deed. Its servant leaders both model and point the way.

During such experiences, servant leaders learn just how important spiritual guidance is. As announced in the Servant Songs, the Servant knows when to give a word that uplifts and encourages. Servant leaders learn when it is important to call attention to the vision. Servant leaders give themselves to what is most important and continually ask where in the midst of all that is happening, they can serve best.

Servant leaders give helpful guidance to people in new endeavors of ministry. Such leaders know when someone needs a rest to renew. They can then slow the pace and join them in celebrating relaxation and refreshment.

Leadership is more than a random act. It is purposeful. There is integrity. There is consistency. In the ups and

Take My Hand

It's nice to know, we are welcome in this place,
To feel at home, to see a smiling face.
Encouragement is hard to find,
When competition is the game
then someone's left behind—

Take my hand, and we will walk together,
For it's hard to go alone—
Everyone needs a friend.
Through our God, we'll be friends forever,
Brothers, sisters, all are one—
With love there is no end.

Each of our lives is a roller-coaster ride.
Who takes the time to really look inside?
All I need to hear is "You're O.K."
And that will give me all the strength
I need to find my way...

We'll walk in the light, as He is in the light,
We'll walk by faith—
By faith and not by sight...
Take my hand, and we will walk together,
For it's hard to go alone—

written for the Junior High Youth · April 1997
by Lynne Grubb Hockley

downs, there is focus. In terms of renewal, rather than setting lofty goals that potentially lead to letdown, servant leaders help establish a plan that often comes in steplike fashion, one small step at a time.

Servant leaders begin where we are and then use vision to help mold the future. Servants point to the kingdom, to be a light to the nations. At the center is the spiritual. Servant leaders lead others to the Living Fountain and join others at the Living Springs that come bubbling up, even unto eternal and real life.

The Biblical Text

One key to this whole process of spiritual movement—upward, inward, and outward—is finding a biblical text that speaks clearly to us regarding renewal. In the next chapter, we will study a text as an example of how such a passage can be explored in depth. From its message, we will hear a call to renewal and see dynamics for renewal at work in the local church.

The text we will study did motivate this very book. During its formative stages, I came across a Scripture in the Easter season that provided a vision for this resource on servant leadership for church renewal. This passage even inspired the subtitle of this book!

We will plumb the text in depth to see its message for us. We will catch its vision of the servant becoming the leader and see the dynamics for renewal in the church. All this is to be unpacked from a lesser-known and perhaps surprising and powerful interlude in the book of Revelation, to which we will turn.

3
Shepherds by the Living Springs

For the Lamb in the midst of the throne
will be their shepherd,
and he will guide them
to springs of living water.
(Rev. 7:17)

In teaching servant leadership and church renewal, I encourage pastors and church leaders to find key biblical texts for renewal that tug at them. In this chapter I illustrate how to use such texts as guides in renewal. This does not mean that you necessarily should use this particular text or that these are the only dynamics for church renewal. Each servant leader should find their own text; each church should envision its own renewal plan.

While preaching from the texts in the lectionary during the Easter season, I discovered a major image of servant leadership in a rather unexpected place: the book of Revelation. Revelation 7:9-19 is a beautiful affirmation of church renewal in an adverse culture. It falls between the opening of the sixth and seventh seal of the scroll recording the purposes of God for the future (Rev. 5:1; Ezek. 2:9-10). In this pause, the author points the eyes of the faithful toward victory.

The Lamb becomes the Shepherd and leads them to springs of living water. What an imagery of the servant becoming the leader! In John's vision for the church of his day, we see broader implications for servant leadership as it relates to church renewal.

From this text we can draw four dynamics of renewal that give fundamental clues to practical renewal in the church. These dynamics of renewal are worship, inner transformation, servant leadership, and spiritual nurture. In other words, in the midst of the need for renewal, servant leadership lifts up the gift of praise, the inner transformation of the heart, the Lamb becoming the Shepherd, and the gift of new life found at the Living Springs. We will explore each of these dynamics as we study this text and its meanings for the church today.

The lectionary compilers list Revelation 7 to be read during the period after Easter and before Pentecost. Known as the great fifty days, this Easter season used to be the central focus of the Christian Year. It was a great time of renewal, the season for baptisms, a time for the church to move from ashes to fire, from Lent to Pentecost.[16] Would not every church leader desire that?

The author of Revelation knew the cost of such discipleship. "I John, your brother, who share with you in Jesus the tribulation and the kingdom and the patient endurance, was on the island called Patmos on account of the word of God and the testimony of Jesus" (Rev. 1:9). Leaving aside debates about author, images, and structure, we know that here is a book intended by its author to encourage early Christians during a time of hardship and persecution. Revelation is a book about victory in the face of defeat. The faithful are triumphant.

Revelation is about the church called to be a new order in the midst of a chaotic culture. In that age, as in any age, the church has a particular challenge and calling to swim upstream, to live by sacred values in a secular world, to hold to a faith when otherwise the cost of discipleship seems too dear. Revelation's message rings through the years: "Don't give up! God is sheltering you. You have a mission. Hold to your vision!"

The author reveals his unique perspective on renewal. There is victory for the faithful. There is new life for old forms. Confined because of his faith, John nonetheless is a fellow laborer in the church. He has shared the tribulation and the kingdom, the ups and downs of living faithfully in the world. Enduring patiently has carried him through the hard times.

His description of himself is short: "servant," which literally means "slave" (Rev. 1:1, Greek: *doulos*). Although a prisoner, here is one who so freely serves Jesus that he is in a position to receive revelation. Servants live by listening and learning and following. John delineates what it means to live in Jesus Christ.[17] Here is his point of identification and affiliation.

From the isle of Patmos, John gives messages to each of seven churches in Asia Minor (Rev. 2–3). His messages speak right to the heart of renewal in the church. John's fear is that the churches will lose their vitality from not keeping up their faith in hard times. When false teachers come, when expectancy of reward is lost, and when complacency overtakes—John's chief concern is for churches to keep their living relationship to Christ. In effect, he says, "Look heavenward, but always remember that you are part of this story."[18]

Starting at Revelation 4, we see unfolding a wonderful mural that tells of the movement of God in the hearts of God's people. In the throne room of God, the Lamb, sent by God to suffer persecution on behalf of humankind, is privileged to open the seals of the scroll telling of God's purposes being worked out. Each seal reveals evils of the present age. Coming later is the ultimate victory of the exalted Christ.

No one in heaven or on earth could open the scroll, except for the Lamb. The Lamb is the one who redeems men and women on earth.[19] God's Servant redeems (Mark 10:45; Rev. 15:3). That is the role of a servant. No wonder we can turn to this passage for an exposition of servant leadership!

This whole interlude of prophetic illumination comes on the Lord's day (Rev. 1:10). John gives a "state of the church" evaluation for each of seven churches. Then he expands his vision of the glory of God and also of judgments for the unrighteous, revealed as the scroll is progressively unsealed. John gives encouragement to the faithful, who need the support of new life when the odds seem against the church.

Let us look at four aspects of new life or dynamics of renewal that stand out in Revelation.

Worship: Praising and Adoring God

"All the angels stood round the throne and round the elders and the four living creatures, and they fell on their faces before the throne and worshiped God" (Rev. 7:11).

The first dynamic for renewal seen in this chapter is worship. Like an organist who plays an interlude before the last verse of a hymn, John makes a break between the opening of the sixth and seventh seals. The continuity in the melody of this great symphony we call Revelation is the vision of the Lamb, the Servant. For one author, this is the vision that sets John the prisoner free: "Freedom is a condition of the soul. It is available to everyone who shifts the focus of his or her life from earth to heaven, from self to God and the Lamb, from time to eternity."[20]

In this interlude, the redeemed, from all tribes and all peoples and all languages, gather to stand before the throne and the Lamb (Rev. 7: 9). They are clothed in white robes, vestments of purification and righteousness (Rev. 19:8; vestment wearers, note protocol!). The faithful have palm branches of victory in their hands.

They are crying out with a loud voice, "Salvation belongs to our God who sits upon the throne, and to the Lamb" (Rev. 7:10). This is a hymn of rejoicing. The faithful, all the servants of God, joined by the elders and the living creatures (angelic beings representing humans and beasts; Ezek. 1:5-10) fall on their faces before the throne of God. They worship and join in singing a beautiful sevenfold doxology, "Amen! Blessing and glory and wisdom and thanksgiving and honor and power and might be to our God for ever and ever! Amen" (Rev. 7:12).

Worship is at the heart of being faithful servants in the kingdom of God. Worship is the way the faithful have always stayed close to the life created by God.[21]

One place to begin the process of renewal is worship, as Marcia Bailey decided at Mayfair Conwell Church. She began with a preaching series that led to a retreat, a children's choir, and the gaining of new members.[22]

Then a pastoral change occurred. I wondered how renewal could continue from one leader to another. In an inspirational installation service, the children's choir surrounded the new pastor and sang! What a way for renewal to continue—through the "new song" of children!

The congregation continues with a new ministry involving twenty families from the neighborhood who had no church. Four or five months later, that ministry has expanded to one hundred new families. A kingdom vision is becoming reality at Mayfair Conwell Church. All this renewal was initiated through a preaching series on worship!

Renewal breaks out when leaders understand that they drink at the same fountains as the people. Leaders share with those who in Jesus know the tribulation and the kingdom and the patient endurance. With that perspective, our preaching contains the good news (gospel) of freedom in Jesus Christ. Our singing is done as the saints who gather around the throne and sing sevenfold doxologies with the angels. Our corporate prayers change as the redeemed thank God and come in confession, absolution, challenge, and dedication.[23]

Renewal is experienced in a new song sung from our hearts. As we begin to form an actual plan of renewal, worship can be a concrete way in which to build the fervency and faithfulness envisioned by John.

Worship is part of what we called "the movement upward" in chapter 2. Renewal always begins with responding to God's love and grace. This is the upward turn. It may take some time to enter into this upward process—and timing is important. John shows this by placing the interlude between the sixth and seventh seals. When the dynamic is right, we must step back and raise our voices in praise. Here is worship at its best. Servant leadership must be attuned to this "pause" in which to thank and praise God for evidences of grace.

Worship, therefore, is the first dynamic of renewal in this passage. Renewal is experienced in a new song sung from our hearts. "Holy, holy, holy, all the saints adore thee.[24] When a congregation begins to respond to God's love and grace, they sing this hymn in a whole new way. Rather than just repeating words, they sing with fervency and meaning. The congregation truly begins to adore God.

Pointing to the author of life, the saints praise the Giver of all, proclaiming, "Victory to our God who sits on the throne, and to the Lamb!" (Rev. 7:10, NEB). Servant leaders can look for such a movement as a sign of a congregation at worship. With such worship experienced, renewal is known by the inner transformation of our hearts, the next topic.

Transformation in the Lamb

"They have washed their robes and made them white in the blood of the Lamb" (Rev. 7:14).

A second part of this interlude in Revelation celebrates the redemptive function of the Lamb. Like a symphony that returns again and again to a central theme, John in his vision returns over and over to the Lamb.

The vision from heaven is that earthbound people are cleansed, not by their own doing, but by the sacrifice of the Lamb. The Lamb mediates covenant. At the heart of the servant leader is one's understanding of redemption and transformation. God redeems; God restores. White robes come from being cleansed in the blood of the Lamb.

Transformation becomes such a crucial thing for John—and for us all today. In John, the servant attempts to demonstrate the unconditional love of God. The faithful people are those who have experienced transformation.

The basic Greek word for the people who gather around the throne is *laos* (Rev. 7:9; eight other uses in the book). From it we derive the word *laity*. John holds no second-class citizenship for them. These people join with the angels in this chorus.

They have experienced and received God's transforming grace. So touched are the cleansed people that they serve day and night in the temple (Rev. 7:15). They are no longer enslaved by evil powers. Now they are rejoicing servants of God. All are a part of the team of saints singing praise to God.

This process of transformation is an integral part of servant leadership. Servants have caught the vision of God's unconditional love. They may not always accept a person's performance, but they will never stop loving and encouraging that person. Their goal is to take imperfect people and help them grow and mature in Christ.

Servant leaders help individuals become even more of what they can be with their God-given talents. Servanthood is recognized for working to help others grow taller in faith and service. As we will see, servant leaders help people form a team with others.

For John, transformation occurs as individuals so attune themselves to Christ that they become one with Christ and Christ's purposes. This is what we call being "in Christ Jesus." In Revelation, John's vision is for earthly people to experience a whole new existence. For John, that means patient endurance, holding steadfastly to Christ through the ups and downs of living faithfully. Maturity in faith means living *now* the victory of Jesus that is to be completed.

To be "in Christ" means having an existence that enjoys the quality of life of the resurrected Christ in the present.[25] Those who are "in Christ" experience that God is with us now. In the Old Testament, the Israelites enjoyed the *Shekinah,* the protective presence of God dwelling with them. In Revelation, the faithful experience the protection of God. The One "who sits upon the throne will shelter them with his presence" (Rev. 7:15). A literal translation suggests that God spreads his tabernacle over his people.

I had the joy of seeing real transformation occur at the Bush Creek Congregation, where I did my doctor of ministry program. Faith transformation, whether for long-term members or new friends, was an extended process. Often it happened among people after they had been connected with the congregation for some time.

Typically I would help new people meet suitable members in the congregation so they found some congenial points of contact and identification. Once people began talking to one other, they felt that they had gained friends with whom they could comfortably share their thoughts and feelings. They had friends to whom they could turn with faith-related questions.

Usually individuals would give evidence of further transformation by becoming more involved or involved again. They might take up some tasks or show interest in other people. A lot of leadership is needed at this point to facilitate interest. Servant leaders are continually opening doors for others in new relationships. As this happens, people gain a new sense of being loved by God and others.

If they are not members, they may begin to think about baptism and ask further questions or decide to make a recommitment to faith and membership. This may be a time for them to take a class on beliefs or to enter some type of discussion group on faith.

When individuals experience this transformation in Christ, some type of service of baptism or reconsecration or reception into membership is held. A sponsor or other person may be a partner in this process. However, the process should not end here. Individuals need to keep growing in faith. Often by that time they are in some group in the church or are finding their way into leadership positions. A commitment grows within them to take some initiative.

They need continued support as they experience the ups and downs that John the Revelator knew so well. Assimilation into the church is an ongoing process of helping people connect more deeply with God and with others.

Servant leaders are aware of the importance of this transformation, not only in individuals, but also in the life of a congregation. As we explore how Revelation 7 might be used to inspire a plan for renewal, we can look at ways in which grace can become real for people.

Moments of silence in a worship service can provide space in which God's grace is experienced and God's protection becomes real. Such times of transformation may occur during a teaching moment in a class or small group. Sometimes members are emotionally and spiritually touched while carrying their ministry into daily life. Servant leaders monitor such transformation.

This is the inward movement of renewal spoken about in chapter 2. The church, transformed by God's love, becomes a community of healing and wholeness for others. Such a movement occurs as people become more attuned to Christ and enter a continuous and deepening process of inner growth. Trust grows, and Christian love pervades more and more in the fellowship.

Servant leaders are attuned to this movement and nurture it, just as John writing from Patmos encouraged early believers to be faithful in their day and time. John knew that

God's presence was hovering over them. Servant leaders help others know that they do not stand on the outside but on the inside of God's love and mercy.

In hardship, John knew what sustained him, and he encouraged others to be confident of the same. To be in Jesus Christ was his point of identification and affiliation. Growing in discipleship is a process of maturing in both the agony and the ecstasy. In the church, such support can come in many forms, including small groups.[26] Shepherds know that the flock needs to have support in the midst of hardships. The people need to be assured that God's victory and protection are with them.

Servant Leader:
The Lamb Becomes the Shepherd

"For the Lamb in the midst of the throne will be their shepherd, and he will guide them to springs of living water" (Rev. 7:17).

One of the most beautiful portions of Revelation, I believe, is where the author John speaks of the Lamb becoming the Shepherd. The Servant becomes the leader. Truly there is a reversal, where the least becomes the greatest. Indeed the Lamb, who carries John's vision from defeat to victory, is chief among those who serve and then lead.

Not by kingly authority but by self-sacrifice, the shepherd watches over others.

On some high moor, across which at night hyenas howl, when you met him sleepless, far-sighted, weather-beaten, armed, leaning on his staff, and looking out over his scattered sheep, every one on his heart, you understand why the shepherd of Judea sprang to the front in his people's history; why they gave his name to their king, and made him the symbol of Providence; why Christ took him as the type of self-sacrifice.[27]

Throughout the ages, servant leaders have demonstrated by their lives how the Lamb becomes the Shepherd. One modern-day example is Mother Teresa. Once the annual conference of the Church of the Brethren met in Charlotte, North Carolina, soon after her visit there. Our family noted aspects of her presence as recorded in the newspaper.

Rather than sleeping in a luxurious hotel, Mother Teresa slept on a cot in a newly established convent. On the card distributed when she met with people, it was noted that no offering would be taken at that evening gathering. People liked her. They sought her out for her spiritual presence; many went to her for spiritual support and guidance.

After eighteen Mennonites traveled to visit Mother Teresa in Calcutta, an article reported how they found evidence of such spiritual nurture. Mother Teresa explained to them what is behind the special mission of her Missionaries of Charity. "All religious congregations take vows of poverty, chastity, and obedience, but in our congregation we take a fourth: to give wholehearted service to the poorest of the poor," she told them.

"No salary; no government grant. We are like the birds and flowers, . . . completely in God's hand. It's a miracle of God. I have never had to send anyone away because I didn't have anything."[28] Mother Teresa was truly a servant leader.

On a local congregational level, where do we find servant leaders? In conducting a study of successful Sunday schools in four believers church traditions, I explored what made for their unique vitality.[29] Here were growing Sunday schools, healthy models of the church.

The title of the study was changed midway because a district member of the Mennonite Church, Dorothy Harnish, suggested that in the believers church tradition, we work for inner transformation of faith in adults, who in turn become role models for children and youths. We wanted to identify factors that made these Sunday schools such vibrant, life-changing places for people.

One of the factors that soon caught my attention was the special people who played key roles. Each made a difference in the spiritual journey of others in their congregation. At one church someone was unusually called "candy man." The children flocked around him—not just for the candy, but because this man had developed such close relationships with the children. They just wanted to be with him. When the candy man was away, the church leaders had to appoint a temporary replacement! This man played a unique role in spiritual nurture of the church's children.

Similarly, in each of the other congregations where I've worked, certain people have played such key roles. They were not known for their prominence. In fact, they were noted as ordinary people. Each one simply had a deep spiritual life and a love for others and thereby played a unique and important role. One was a man who visited all the families of the kindergarten class. This became a special endeavor known to all. Families waited eagerly for the time when their child would be in that class. As a side benefit, teacher turnover in the department was low.

In another Brethren in Christ congregation was a farming family. Even though they were busy with their labors on the farm, they had special relationships with people and helped with programs in the church. In another church, servant leaders clearly stood out. One individual was continually finding ways to affirm other people. He regularly lifted up the value of diversity and spoke of the importance of individuals who made a real difference.

Concerned that they not rest on their laurels, he would always encourage them to move into the future. It was a delight to be at meetings he attended. No one had to tell me who was the true leader for the group! Through such servant leaders, people felt supported and were growing day by day.

Another much-larger congregation had a unique shepherding program that had been established by a former pastor, sensitive to the needs of people. The congregation is divided up into shepherding groups that meet regularly for prayer and mutual support. Between meetings they call each other concerning special needs of members.

In addition, all the group shepherds meet as a leading team on Sunday mornings during part of the Sunday school hour. It is evident what a positive impact this shepherding program makes on the congregation!

It is clear that, as they serve, all of these people mentioned above have become leaders. They convey God's sheltering by their presence. They provide spiritual nurture by their actions and words. They lead people by fountains of living waters. Often their stories are untold. But as one inquires into what nurtures and strengthens their congregations, their hidden stories become known.

In a real sense, John's vision for the early church still applies to today's church. If you are seeking renewal for your congregation, identify the servants who are busy doing what they do best—serving, caring about people—without seeking fame or recognition.

This is the third movement outward in joy and service. For transformation to occur in the church, we move outward in God's Spirit. Even though we feel we are not capable, as servants we realize that our call is to be used by God. God uses imperfect people to do God's work. Our efforts can seem so inadequate against all that needs to be done. Yet by following the lead of God's Spirit, we can follow the way of Christ into servanthood.

When we follow the Spirit, God will accomplish through unlikely servants the tasks God wants to perform. Through this very process, servants grow in faith. They find that they grow in faith by serving the needs of others.

This is John's vision for leadership in the church—and our third dynamic. The Lamb, weak, defenseless, and vulnerable, is focused on mediating for God. God can use unlikely people in the congregation to bring about transformation and change. Simple folk, like the candy man, can help change the lives of people.

The unlikely can serve on behalf of others and lift them up in faith and courage. As we saw in the opening of the seals, the Lamb is the one who mediates for God and points people to the throne. The Lamb serves on behalf of others and lifts them up. They receive salvation through the Lamb and shelter with God. In Christ's victory, the Lamb becomes the Shepherd.

Sharing at the Living Springs

"The Lamb . . . will guide them to springs of living water; and God will wipe away every tear from their eyes" (Rev. 7:17). What a beautiful close to this interlude! The Lamb-become-Shepherd now leads the people to the springs of living water. Here is where refreshment and renewal can continually occur.

What shepherds know is that they need to drink from the living waters of God and lead others to those fountains of self-renewing life. Out of this renewal comes the basis of creativity for ministry, courage in hardship, and joy in times of sadness. We drink at the fountains, and God wipes away tears.

Renewal is crucial for successful servant leaders, both for themselves and for those they are leading. For those being led, it means their spiritual needs are being met. So many people in our society realize how much they hunger for meaning. They seek for a place where they will be cared for genuinely. They seek a place of authentic spiritual depth. They seek a place where there is shelter.

For renewal to occur in a congregation, such experiences must be a regular part of their lives. Out of renewal also comes a vision for leadership as well as creativity for ministry. From being renewed comes a fresh look at fellow Christians and a vibrant plan for ministry.

So much of what one does in leadership is best formulated in times of refreshment down by the springs. In discerning God's will and intent, in drawing back from action to reflection, in receiving God's power and strength, we are assured of God's shelter and presence. Spiritual renewal is what keeps leaders and other believers focused on the Shepherd.[30]

Servant leaders often return to the springs, for spiritual renewal, gaining a vision, identifying strengths, matching needs and strengths, setting goals, or establishing a renewal plan. By centering themselves spiritually, servant leaders find direction to lead. They lead by following the Shepherd. This can be done alone or with the renewal committee of co-leaders from the congregation and with others who are on the walk of faith.

This renewing of leadership continues, not just in the planning for renewal, but also in the implementation. One may be training people for ministry, doing the supervision process or encouraging people in the renewal process. Through it all, the ongoing spiritual renewal of leaders gives them the hunches and urges to do the work.

Such renewal can happen during board meetings, while one is cleaning up the churchyard, or when helping on a service project in the community. It can also happen in one's home, at the place of one's employment, and on the volleyball court.

I learned in a special way that spiritual renewal needs to be owned by a church and by its members. The Bush Creek congregation worked with me to formulate a list of goals. They listed personal spiritual growth as top priority for the pastor and congregation.[31]

We invited a group of leaders from elsewhere to visit our congregation and help us establish a lay witness mission. The first weekend was successful, so we decided to host a second such weekend visit, but it was a great letdown.

Through that experience, members discovered that they

had to find their own way of being renewed. So the church owned the process and established a faith retreat weekend. Through this they discovered a servant style of working at spiritual renewal with an open, inviting spirit to help others grow.

Along with the movements upward, inward, and outward comes a whole way of being sustained by the song in one's heart—like the Servant Songs of Second Isaiah. Effective ministry begins within the heart of the servant so sustained by the song that the way of God is pointed to in all the servant does. This has been called "ministering out of the overflow."[32]

In the process of congregational renewal, servants learn how important this inner renewal is both for themselves and for others. Leaders need to be sustained by the springs of living water, just as do other people.

Before looking at how we ready a congregation for renewal, let us check what John means by "springs" and "living water." In Revelation 7:17, John closes his interlude by pointing to "springs," "fountains of living water." The Greek word here for springs is *"pēgē"* (PAY-gay), the same word John uses in his Gospel for the water drawn by the woman at the well and for the water of "eternal life" that Jesus would give (John 4:6, 14). Rather than standing pools of water that can be depleted, fountains or springs are everbubbling sources of life.

Biblically, water is a symbol for life itself, given by God (Ps. 107:33-38). As a term, *water* can be used for physical sustenance. Yet we have an extension of that in John's Gospel. Life-giving water from Jesus is ever bubbling up to eternal life. One can partake of such renewing for life right now, not just in the future.

The Old Testament was preparing the spiritual meaning carried by an image of water springing up to bring future salvation and renewal. Second Isaiah reports the Lord's resolve to do "a new thing; now it springs forth. . . . I will make a way in the wilderness and rivers in the desert" (43:19). The Lord as the Shepherd of Israel (40:11) "will lead them, and by springs of water will guide them" (49:10). According to Jeremiah, the Lord even calls himself "the fountain of living waters," forsaken by Israelite evildoers (2:13; 17:13). In the future, living waters would flow forth from the house of the Lord and water the valley year-round (Ezek. 47; Joel 3:18; Zech. 14:8). *Living waters* thus becomes a symbol for salvation from the Lord.

Eventually Jesus makes the great claim that he himself can give this "spring of water welling up to eternal life" (John 4:14). He says that those who drink from him can themselves have "rivers of living water" flowing from their hearts. The Evangelist interprets this to refer to Jesus giving the Spirit to believers, who then share spiritual waters of life with others (John 7:37-39).

Thus, through Jesus Christ and the Spirit he gives, eternity renews us for the present and the future. Certainly the term *Living Springs* in the vision of Revelation holds the same image that being "in Christ" does. In abiding fellowship with Christ, we are refreshed by the living water.[33]

In the New Testament, Jesus is the Good Shepherd who cares for the sheep (Mark 6:34; John 10:1-18; Heb. 13:20; cf. Ps. 23). Servant leaders are under-shepherds, called to pastor and love and care for Christ's flock, serving the chief Shepherd and accountable to him (John 21:15-17; Acts 20:28; 1 Pet. 5:1-4; 2:25).

The shepherds by these springs (Rev. 7:17) are servant leaders who know the constant source of their own renewal. Living waters are not cistern waters—stagnant, contaminated, impure, or running dry. What makes for renewal in the church is leading others to the ever-renewing water that brings life.[34] It is from these springs that servant leaders lead.

Realizing that continual refreshment is part of the walk of living in Christ, servants rise in faith to do all the things that leadership is called upon to do. From that vantage, we will look at a variety of leadership doings. Meanwhile, we know that we are shepherds by the Living Springs, ever partaking of and leading others to the waters of the living Christ.

For this fourth dynamic from our Scripture, servant leaders keep pointing toward the fountains of spiritual refreshment. This can happen during a devotional time, a spiritual retreat, a time for leaders to refresh. Servant leaders know the value of such pauses. For renewal to occur, such planned and unplanned moments encourage us to join Jesus at the well. Yet renewal is not just putting on programs. This dynamic points to the fountains that refresh, living water from Christ, given through the Spirit of God.

Each of the dynamics we've just explored—worship, transformation, servant leadership, and spiritual nurture—can help us in developing a renewal plan. Renewal can entail all four dynamics. Some may turn into programming; others may be an emphasis running through the whole church life. All four dynamics can keep us attuned to God's Spirit as we explore such themes.

A solid biblical focus, directed by dynamics of renewal from a chosen key text, can keep propelling us toward our mission and our vision, as assigned by God. All of our planning can then take on a focus. We continue to go deeper into the chosen text as we put our plans into action. We will see how these dynamics can point to areas of renewal in the church. In it all, transformation becomes real in our lives.

4

Servant Leadership and Approaching Renewal

In "A Meditation on the Church: Ice, Water, and Pickup Trucks," Stephen Dintaman tells the story of Garrison Keillor ice fishing. Garrison, known from his radio program, *A Prairie Home Companion*, enjoyed spending nights out with the men fishing on the frozen lake. However, he had a fear: the men would drive their pickup trucks out onto the ice. Ten-inch ice was likely strong enough, but Garrison also knew how heavy the trucks were. Could the ice hold them up?

At this point he needed his perception to be changed. Garrison was relieved to learn that actually it was not the ice that supported the trucks and the fishermen, but the water underneath the ice. The ice only distributes the weight.[35] His relief came in a change of perception and understanding.

In a similar way, servant leadership helps release the body from fear of the unknown by providing the guidance needed to effect renewal. Servant leaders remind people by all they say and do that it is God's presence and strength and power that sustain the church. After listening to their concerns, servant leaders try to help people relate to their faith, their sense of vision, and their calling.

Servant leadership is therefore at the heart of renewal. It helps people discover how and where they can use their gifts in service to God and to others. It helps the congregation gain confidence that God will sustain them. By preparing themselves first, servant leaders can help a congregation or district embark on a period of new growth and vitality.

How can servant leaders prepare themselves? Before giving reading lessons, teachers usually test children for reading readiness. So also in renewal, the development of a certain readiness is needed. We must know that God is with us—calling us, leading us, and sustaining us. In this chapter we will look in depth at the steps servant leaders need to take to prepare themselves for renewal.

Listening to God

The first job of servant leaders is listening. In Isaiah we saw how God opens the servant's ears daily. Listening begins with discerning what God is saying and what God's people are saying.

To gain a sense of God's direction, the servant leader must spend good time in prayer, in listening to God. This is where all of renewal in service begins.

My best ideas for church renewal begin with my own prayer discipline. At the office, I like first to check the Scripture passage I am currently reading. I read a number of verses. Then I reflect on how the Scripture speaks to my life. I write a prayer in my journal, and I think of how this passage speaks to me.

Sometimes I read a meditation. Often during that day, I find myself facing the same issue and being guided by that passage. Insofar as I follow the guidance of the Scripture, my life is lived out of the Word for that day.

Similarly, as you approach church renewal, listening in prayer is crucial. Rather than rushing in with big plans and self-made goals, the servant leader can begin to hear how God is speaking in this situation. What strengths are present? What needs are evident? How can we find a fuller sense of God's presence in this situation? Where can we now serve? To discern how God is moving and working, servant leaders begin from within.

Our listening also includes listening to people, both

what they are saying and what they are not saying. What affirmations are present? What needs are evident? What strengths are present? Those strengths are often indicators of where God is present. Talents are evidences of God at work in people's lives.

Listening is an effective tool to get a handle on the strengths of a situation. When servant leaders listen, people feel that their leaders are with them. People can sense when they are heard. Then the walls come down between people, and they know God is moving and working among them.

Listening paid a large dividend for a servant leader on a special Monday evening at the Frazer Mennonite Church in Malvern, Pennsylvania. I had the dual role of conducting a Bible study on James[36] and teaching the congregation the renewal process.

That evening after some teaching, I had the people break into the usual small groups. I asked them to share their unique strengths as well as where they had been nurtured spiritually[37] (see worksheet 4). In the process of debriefing the groups before the whole congregation, I found that the people had caught a vision (cf. Prov. 29:18, KJV). Excited, they then told what they had learned about their strengths, which clearly focused on offering mutual support.

I listened intently to what the people had to say. Many of them were in caring professions and therefore often in a role of supporting other individuals. Some of them were social workers. I was reminded of the closing chapter of James (5:13-20), where God's help is invoked in the anointing, in the context of mutual support of the faith community.

The phrase "The Healing Community" kept coming to mind. I shared with them, from the perspective of James, the concept of a church taking on the role of being with people spiritually and emotionally. We shared a bit more and went home. I was unable to return the next night because I had a severe case of bronchitis.

Out of this one meeting, the congregation gathered and

formed an exciting vision statement. They had excellent dialogue to explore the meaning of what they felt drawn to do in sharing healing. They concluded that "Frazer Mennonite Church is a Compassionate Community walking with Christ toward peace and wholeness." They began printing this statement in their Sunday bulletins and immersing themselves in their vision through sermons by the pastor. Everyone was exposed to the mission statement, and many began living it out.

When I met with the elders of the congregation some three years later, they told me how much gaining a vision had changed them. Even before putting a plan for renewal in place, they experienced new excitement and vitality. People in the congregation would spontaneously and enthusiastically stand up during their Sunday worship time to tell their stories. New people, who are looking for such a supportive fellowship, have come and have been drawn in, just because the church's mission is clear. This is before any program or special emphasis has begun. Having the mission clear has made all the difference.

Servant leaders learn to listen well. Besides having a congregation gather in small groups, a servant leader can listen to people by visiting them in their homes. I have seen this done effectively by pastors, deacons, and other leaders. Visiting provides an excellent opportunity to see people in their natural environment. People are usually more relaxed in their homes, and visitors can observe others' talents and interests firsthand. Visiting provides a way to encourage people in their faith journey.

There are some fundamental rules in visitation, however. One key is that this visit is for this family's benefit. The servant leader does not use a general visitation appointment to ask someone to do something or to tell someone how to do something. Unless otherwise negotiated, visiting is an opportunity to offer encouragement to people in their ministry.

Through listening, servant leaders can help people identify their talent and affirm what they feel good about in their service to Christ. Visitors can also assess their strengths and needs for ministry. Before leaving, the visitor can offer a closing prayer, invoking God's presence and guidance around the variety of experiences that have been shared.

Servant leaders have the responsibility to listen. Whether in small groups or with one other person, listening can often call forth the gifts of others. Listening provides support for people as they explore their own yet-unnamed gifts. Listening provides encouragement for those who offer themselves in service. Listening provides the means whereby one begins to serve.

Often it all begins in one's prayer life as the servant leader listens to the movement of God. God's Spirit then spills out as we listen to God's movement among people.

Motivating the People

Executives, pastors, and church leaders alike often struggle with the question "How can we motivate people?" Sometimes it seems that no one has the time to do anything. Attendance lags at church, and something seems to be wrong. Someone will suggest that priorities are in the wrong place. Another member may say that people lack a sense of commitment. Soon everyone realizes that we don't improve the situation by sitting around and discussing what is not. What can we do?

First, our question is misguided. We do not do the motivating. Only God can do that. We can get into endless frustration by thinking we can motivate. Servant leaders, shepherds by the Living Springs, know that it is the springs that refresh; from that source, we serve and lead. Preparing for renewal means living with the expectancy that something important is happening. As we drink of the waters, our excitement will grow.

In class after class, in church after church, I have seen a

shift occur when servant leaders begin to listen to God and to others, as described above. This is especially true when it comes to identifying congregational strengths, which is usually done best through a simple exercise. Two questions are asked of the congregation: Where is your spiritual life nurtured in this congregation? What are the strengths of your church?

Behind these two questions is perhaps another. What factors could we build on for new growth? How might we then serve with our strengths and talents? Often after this exercise is done, I see a shift that motivates the heart. Servant leaders see the importance of this shift.

After this exercise is completed, people often become highly motivated. Servant leaders, who know the importance of this shift, can help discern where God is speaking and where the potential for growth is strongest. By identifying people's strengths, we recognize God-given talents at work in each unique situation.

Often people share untold stories. I have seen tears come to people's eyes as they share with others what or who has helped them. Congregations don't regularly do this together; when they do, the energy level goes up. People are free to identify what is important and what is vital, not only for themselves, but also for others. From here, a vision becomes clearer. One may well incorporate this congregational experience as part of the formation of a vision statement.

I have also seen church leaders and pastors move from frustration and discouragement to new excitement and energy through such a process. Spiritual life and growth are of prime importance to most church leaders. But church activities may become so routine and mundane that they expect little to happen. They can subtly convey that lack of expectancy to others.

By pointing to what is valuable and timeless, leaders unlock the strengths of their congregation—and often see their own hearts transformed as well. The spiritual life that is so crucial can then come to the fore.

In sharing about strengths and where people have touched one another's lives, we discover, however, that there is a gap between what is present and what is needed or what is possible. Identifying the gap need not be discouraging; it can help people see what is needed.[38]

We don't want to put people down or make them feel inadequate because of what has already happened. Instead, an affirmative approach can lift up their strengths, celebrate where they have nurtured one another, and help them identify God's specific call in their lives. The church can begin to agree on a vision. They can foresee themselves taking part in a meaningful future.

This very turnaround in motivation happened at the Bush Creek Church of the Brethren as we became more intentional about our work as a church. We began to respond to discerned needs and people began to feel included. As a result, their motivation increased.

We recognized that motivation arose from the very heart of the individual; it is not just an operational process. As people began to connect their faith journey with their ministry of service, they began to feel part of something significant happening in their church—and in their lives.[39]

A renewal team may want to look at the whole motivational issue, both for the church and for themselves. They can begin by asking how they are going to be renewed themselves to carry out their task of church renewal. For that reason, when they meet they should have a significant time of prayer. They need to seek God's leading.

The renewal team may choose to have a spiritual retreat of their own where the agenda is laid aside and people are allowed just to partake of the Living Springs. The spiritual renewal team of the Atlantic Northeast District of the Church of the Brethren does this as part of their regular ongoing work.

One function of the renewal team could be to help the

whole congregation develop its prayer life. This could be started on an individual basis. The team may also facilitate a time of retreat for the entire congregation. As part of Bush Creek's vision for a closer walk of faith, the church planned a faith retreat weekend. Many models can be used that include worship, small group sharing, and meals.

Don't be discouraged if some people don't want to attend. Sometimes it will take several years of listening to the excitement of others before certain people decide to attend a retreat. The best way to motivate people is to help them experience what spiritual growth is all about. Be patient; motivation does not always develop overnight— though it may!

Motivation can also emerge as people gain a vision. Vision gives a way for people to capture their faith, their imagination, and their energies. Such a vision, however, needs to be concrete and workable, something people can become a part of. Readying for renewal involves catching such a vision and also catching people's hearts. A vision has to be something that each person can share. It motivates each person into ministry.

The renewal team can play an important role by encouraging others. Rather than thinking about what people won't do, why not encourage them in what they are doing? When someone has done something thoughtful for you that touched you deeply, thank that person. When we are served in such a meaningful way, we feel called up higher (cf. Luke 14:10). We are affirmed. We feel a sense of motivation.

What about the little greeting card that comes on the day when everything has gone upside down? What about a thoughtful phone call in return?

Transformation must happen internally first—before externals can change. In the Servant Songs of Isaiah, the servant leader leads from the heart of peace. From within, there are the indicators for real transformation. Robert Greenleaf says that too many settle for being critics and experts, "retreating into research without seeing task in building institutions as entailing inner work."[40]

At the heart of servant leadership is ministering heart to heart. We motivate others by being models for them—models of servants who are being renewed by the Living Springs.

In servant leadership we discover that we all need to be transformed. We all need to be redeemed from lethargy, self-sufficiency, and pride. It's not just everyone else but *we* who need renewal. To use an analogy from the Lord's Supper (developed later), we all need to have our feet washed. As the Pyrenees sheepdogs grew up with the sheep and knew their own need for water, so we all need to return to the watering springs. Here is where service begins.

Remember the apostle John's vision for the church? The saints are those who had their robes washed in the blood of the Lamb (Rev. 7:14). Transformation and redemption are key in the process. Here is the positive gift of the Lamb, who sacrificed all for us so we could share the victory. Here is what is of such great value. Now our robes are white. We can pick up palm branches and shout and sing!

We have already seen how such transformation in faith is often a long process. People need to learn how to replace one priority with another. They must organize and plan. As the church, we want our experiences to match our growing maturity in faith. Thus transformation becomes an ongoing process through identifying strengths, becoming motivated by a vision, and developing spiritually. Such transformation is a priceless gift!

Carrying the Vision

Servant leaders know they not only need to help a church gain a vision and get motivated spiritually. They also must learn to carry the vision in their hearts.

My book *A New Heart and A New Spirit* offers guidance

on gaining a vision by identifying *strengths*, evident *needs*, and a *biblical calling*. Worksheet 5 of this book shows these three key elements at the angles of a triangle. From each angle, we peer to find a way to the center, which is growth and renewal.

Servant leaders soon learn that they need, not only to develop a vision, but also to carry a vision. This means developing the vision in small stages, building one experience on top of another. Leaders need to lend support to growth that is underway.

Israel was called to be a light to the nations (Isa. 49:6). This didn't happen overnight; adjustment, change, and challenge were necessary. Likewise, ministries take a lot of time to grow and mature. Risk is entailed. Few ministries develop overnight. Patience is required. It is often in the ups and downs that growth occurs. From the setbacks, we learn what doesn't work. A vision can't be seen in its fullness at the start. It grows as we grow in serving.

In carrying a vision, servant leaders realize that a change in self-perception is often needed for the congregation. They must go from feeling worthless and defeated to feeling challenged and excited in their new calling. While it all sounds good, a lot of change is involved—and change can be difficult.

A vision is something one grows into; it is not an instant success. Servant leaders learn all the dynamics that go into their vocation. At each point the servant leader carries the vision. In the ups and downs, one stays faithful to the call, the challenge, and the possibilities.

In forming a youth ministry council at Elizabethtown, we learned as a church how a vision can grow. First, I had to learn again how to conduct a meeting since my work as pastor did not often bring me into that role. I learned to listen well and hard and to include people. As we began formulating a mission statement, we decided to ask the youths for their input. This was an excellent idea, helping to give the youths ownership in the mission statement.

I learned a collaborative approach of drawing together all the strands of ideas. The mission of the group began to grow out of our statement of intent in forming a youth ministry council as an umbrella for youth ministry. In response to calling forth youths as leaders, the group responded favorably to forming a ministerial scholarship fund to help youths enter some kind of full-time ministry vocation.

Servant leaders learn how a vision keeps developing and evolving. It has been said that leaders should work themselves out of a job. There is a certain truth in that statement. Leaders must learn to delegate and turn over tasks of leadership. However, a servant leader plays a crucial role in carrying a vision. Everything the servant leader does keeps the vision growing.

In Robert Greenleaf's earliest monograph, he tells of the mythical hero Leo, who led a group of people.[41] This servant leader had sustained the group with his spirit and his song. However, he had failed to train others in the group to lead. When he dropped out, the group unraveled. Thus, the servant leader plays a crucial role. Leadership is needed to keep the vision growing. That vision becomes a driving force of spirit.

Practical implementation of this is very important. Servant leaders offer encouragement along the way. When someone does something positive to uphold or further the vision, servant leaders make it a point to commend that person for doing a good job. When people have expended a lot of energy in a certain area, thank-you notes can go a long way. In the church, this can also be done through the bulletin or newsletter.

When things don't go so well, servant leaders are there as well. They call someone on the phone and listen as a concern is verbalized. Perhaps a group of people need to get together to talk things over. In this way things are handled before they become large. Rather than letting their feelings fester, people can bring them into the open, process them, and receive counsel.

If comments are dealt with promptly and communication is up to date, negative feelings are less likely to submerge the vision. Servant leaders can help put things into perspective and buoy people up by the spirit of the endeavor. The servant leader moves the initiative along. Others pick up this effort as well.

Servant leaders grow in skills and in spirit as the group grows. I grew while chairing the youth ministry council. I learned how to put the most-important items first at a meeting, how to help the group to come to a decision, and how to ensure that follow-up would be done. When servant leaders invest in the process, they will grow. The vision will grow as well. Often servant leaders may see the unknown risks that carrying a vision entails, such as fatigue. Spiritual rejuvenation will be needed at certain points in the renewal process.

While getting the Elizabethtown youth ministry underway, I used three separate days for quiet spiritual retreat. I found a retreat center and took my Bible and several devotional aids. I spent a lot of time listening, then reading my regular Scriptures for the day, and then reading devotional literature. As a result, I found myself being renewed. I felt strength to keep moving into the vision while all was not yet complete. I gained a real sense that this was God's vision, and that we were being lifted up and strengthened to carry it through.

Earlier we said that servant leaders gain a vision by seeing things whole; they see how things can fit together. While there are no assurances that a vision will be born, servants continually gain insight on what can make things work together. They keep their eye on what can make theirs a more serving community.

How can the church accomplish its goals and serve its vision? How is God using these moments and movements so that the kingdom will come more in its fullness? Servant leaders carry the vision on their hearts.

Calling Forth Leaders

Leaders call forth leaders. Just as servants model how others are to serve, so do servant leaders call others to serve and so to lead. We see that in servant leaders gathering a renewal team. We see that in how they supervise new people learning the way of serving. Servant leaders are team builders. They see leadership skills in others and affirm their strengths.

Servant leaders are continually enlisting leaders. They begin with where people are and build understanding, trust, and support. They help people gain a vision for how they might grow. Jesus held forth a vision as he called his disciples. Each came out of a different background, had different talents, and held varied interests. But Jesus was able to call them forth to use their lives in service to God's purpose.

When servant leaders call forth other servant leaders, they work to build enthusiasm, enlist help, and have others join in the journey. Servant leaders don't begin by just desiring to fill a vacant slot. They see where others can have their talents used for the vision and where they will be fulfilled in their service. They see how others can grow and become more like they were created to be. They foresee how others can grow spiritually in this whole renewal process.

The Akron Church of the Brethren discovered that nurturing leaders was crucial for their growth. A member of the district spiritual renewal team went to the church to encourage the spiritual growth of the congregation. The board drew together some people to host the visitor. Out of that meeting, the congregation decided to call two team members for another meeting. As a result, some more individuals were added to the local renewal team. Deacons, who had the official role of spiritual nurture, composed about half the group.

In a follow-up meeting, one member of the team offered a thoughtful devotional. I was present to help the congregation share about where they had been touched spiritually in the church. We explored their strengths as well. Originally they had various thoughts as to direction for adding programs, but now a new focus emerged. People in this congregation touched one another's lives spiritually by being models, offering support, and having real commitment to each other and the Lord.

That evening we also identified a real core of lay leaders, those who could be nurtured and could serve as a base. This leadership core could be expanded to serve the large number of children and youths. Developing and training lay leaders became top priority.

Out of that evening came a biblical vision from Psalm 100: Serve the Lord with gladness, not sadness. The church went on to talk about what we mean by *renewal*. They then began to get organized.

The Akron church members devoted some time on Sunday morning to look more at what renewal means. They asked me to come and preach. From the Scriptures we looked at renewal as an ongoing process of spiritual growth that keeps renewing us and the church.

Afterward, the church looked at the process that was underway. They decided to slim down some of the organization—a suggestion from the local team to avoid overlap and extra wear on some leaders. Small groups were initiated to continue the spiritual support of members. The group also identified the need to train leaders and expand the leadership base.

During a follow-up meeting, I asked the pastor, Richard Sisco, to offer some thoughts on Psalm 100. He noted how the Psalter presents a new song with new instruments used by the Israelites to express their faith. Richard encouraged the group to serve with a song, to help with a hum, and to work with a whistle. That was made concrete in what followed. Richard had the group first sing the doxology (from Psalm 100), then hum it, and then whistle it. Yes, it can be done. The theme of Psalm 100 came alive!

At that point, we were almost ready to begin building a plan of renewal. Before this part was done, however, and even while seeing some options before us, we reviewed the concepts of servant leadership (see worksheet 6). As a renewal team, we spent quality time looking at how leaders function and at the traits of servant leaders. The team prepared to share about their priorities, which could be mapped out over a period of time. They presented these priorities at the next congregational meeting.

Servant leaders learn how important it is to provide training for people whom they are serving and calling into leadership. So often people feel inadequate—or at least feel that they do not have the proper tools. Where will they begin? Besides, they claim they already have enough to do. Life has a way of filling up with endless TV shows or many relatively good things.

Training for leadership is a good way to bring focus and reset priorities as well as save time. In fact, training could be held on servant leadership throughout the organization. To that could be added training in an individual interest area.

Over the years I have experienced how crucial training is for ministries. I have seen training supplied for ushers, Sunday school teachers, youth leaders, and boards. Good training does not start with all the things I want to have shoved into people. Instead, servant leaders begin with people where they are and then help new servant leaders grow.

This is called teaching by learning objectives: starting with where people are, establishing goals, and figuring out how the people can grow. Then leaders can develop a teaching plan by putting in the steps needed to reach the goals.

As the ministry at Elizabethtown was unfolding, we

identified a training event for youth counselors. Some who were already involved tapped others with perceived potential. We attended a training event at the local parish resource center that was hosting a youth pastor. A certain spirit developed out of that event as we learned what a successful youth ministry looks like. We also looked at practical tools on how to communicate with youths.

For instance, the trainer shared how he cut up cereal boxes and used them as postcards to send notes to youths. He observed that youths like to get mail and they like people to take an interest in them. The combination of philosophy and hands-on illustrations made this a great beginning.

From there, we tapped a capable youth trainer, Walt Mueller.[42] I sat down with him and went over how our youth ministry was evolving. We decided to hold an event for all youths and their parents. Walt wanted to draw the youths and adults into a dialogue about things that mattered to the youths. This provided a way to help them learn how to communicate better with each other.

Out of this arose an opportunity to cosponsor an event at the parish resource center with Walt, who was going to hold a workshop on youths and their culture. Getting leaders involved in training can result in further interest. A momentum begins. A whole spirit develops. Growth comes in this atmosphere of working together.

Calling forth leaders is a whole process, from identification of people with gifts to training them to lead. Servant leaders see how people can be supported in their talents. They can develop an understanding of what leadership involves and provide the actual training necessary. Every area in the life of the church can use training for leadership, both in general and then in specifics.

Many organizations hold regular in-service events, regular training on specific topics. They know that people need tools and training to learn how to serve and lead. Regular training is the way to keep leaders equipped. It can also prevent burnout and rejuvenate those weary of the responsibilities of leadership. A whole spirit of hope and enthusiasm develops when good training is involved. It is exciting for servant leaders to see the vision becoming reality. While setting direction and serving needs sometimes seem like opposites, servant leaders find how one grows out of the other. Both these actions work in sync to renew the church.

In setting the direction for renewal, servant leaders understand how important it is to be attentive to God's leading and in touch with serving the people and their needs. Servant leadership sets us on the road to renewal.

5

Servant Leadership and Organizing for Renewal

Do you remember the Great Pyrenees sheepdogs that bonded with their sheep? They knew their own need for water, yet they always responded to the call of their shepherd and took the sheep with them. Likewise in servant leadership, we must be spiritually sensitive to our Shepherd while also being aware of the talents and needs of others and ourselves.

With the calls of so many voices, how can leaders develop this kind of sensitivity? In the midst of all the activities that seem to be happening, what is leadership? How is servant-style leadership different from any other kind of leadership?

In organizing for renewal, we will see how servant leadership can be an effective model for us. The beautiful imagery of the sheepdogs can help us differentiate between effective and ineffective leadership. For instance, leaders have to be cautious about going ahead on their own and being separate from others.

It also is not wise to call people "sheep" and treat them as though we know best and they don't know what they are doing. When such signals are seen and heard, people's talents, as well as our own talents as leaders, remain unavailable to us.

When servant leaders hear the voice of their loving Shepherd, however, they carefully consider the call and slow down to ponder the message. We will do that in this chapter. Thus we will build a servant-style leadership that provides a solid basis for renewal and speaks the message of the gospel. Clear focus is needed in organizational work. In renewal, servant leaders need to take initiative to further the process and build upon what has already been happening. All the groundwork already laid includes a lot of organizing. So we are not starting from scratch. Such thoughtful work, already established, becomes an integral part of setting the tone for what is to come. Preparation models the renewal process.

We have already seen that leaders can begin the renewal process by growing deeper spiritually themselves. This takes an intentionality that initiates the process of renewal and sustains the leader through the organizing stage.

Being led by the Living Springs is not separated from the other organizational tasks. Instead, they all work together. In this chapter we will look at four areas of organizing: the spiritual work, establishing a renewal plan, anticipation and timing, and implementing renewal ministries.

The Spiritual Work of Organizing

It is easy to forget that organizing is a spiritual work. We are not just establishing some program. Christ is guiding our purpose, and the program to be established is a ministry. Furthermore, pastors keep reminding me that when renewal becomes merely a *program* in people's minds, it is relegated to some committee and forgotten. When renewal is rooted in spiritual growth, and that is where leaders begin, renewal becomes the heart of the church.

Going deeper spiritually keeps the leader in touch with God's guidance. Going deeper spiritually means being able to see the strengths of a congregation and the talents of members. Going deeper spiritually gives the leader sensitivity about the needs to be met. Going deeper spiritually gives the impetus and the power to lead.

Here at the Living Waters, one finds refreshment and joins others in the whole spiritual journey.

The leader's spiritual growth and organizational work should not be separated. In fact, organizing for renewal is mostly a spiritual task, for the leader is seeking the guidance of God and is attempting to build a team of God's people. We also know that the end product as well as the process along the way is to help a church grow deeper spiritually. So servant leaders need to model the desired product, to demonstrate the results.

You would not be a good salesperson for Volvo if you drove a Cadillac into that dealer's parking lot with a prospective customer standing by! On one level, leaders are not salespersons; on another, they should represent the product they are promoting. As leaders "drive" the "model" they are hoping others will become part of, they also learn more about their "model."

If this is more than a job for the salesperson (and customers always can tell), the salesperson had better "own" the car before going on the lot. A leader establishing a car dealership would probably want to teach people about the product, help them grow in appreciation for its merits, and have them drive the model as well. This would allow people to experience the product being promoted.

Therefore, the leader's task is to grow spiritually and to help others grow spiritually as well. This should happen in all that leaders do. If one is looking specifically at organizing for renewal, then this task becomes quite specific. In forming any kind of a committee in renewal, one of the first tasks would be to find people who are growing deeper spiritually or who want to do so. We even want some who would consider this deeper spiritual walk if they only knew how to begin.

So many people welcome the idea of spiritual renewal. They sense this need in their own lives. They feel it in their families. They know the need in their place of employment.

They experience it in their community. They know the global community needs spiritual renewal. They welcome going deeper in faith, both personally and as the church.

One of the tasks of renewal for leadership is to identify ways for people to grow spiritually and to have resources available for others to grow deeper in faith. This is why one forms a renewal team and goes to the deacon body or uses the board of Christian nurture. Even as they are doing mundane organizational tasks, leaders can grow deeper spiritually and help others grow spiritually. Renewal then is not simply a program or a set plan. It is catching God's movement and establishing a vision.

A servant leader may suggest to a renewal team that there be a season of prayer. As there was to be a Sabbath year in Jewish life every seven years, so there could be a year of rest to pray (Lev. 25). One might go to the prayer groups in the congregation and ask for a concentrated time of prayer for renewal. During such a time, the real leaders of a congregation often emerge and renewal begins.[43]

Renewal is finding God's Spirit in our hearts and seeing that a ministry of renewal is ahead. The renewal is not a program once and for all. Instead, it is the beginning of a never-ending process of nurturing the faith in ourselves. We keep building up the body of Christ, and in Christ's name washing the feet of other servants. The spiritual life that leads to serving others reflects an exciting authenticity of faith.

Establishing a Plan for Renewal

We have talked in a preliminary way about envisioning a plan for renewal in a local congregation. We have looked at starting more intentionally into our own spiritual walk, being drawn to a Scripture passage, catching a vision, and building a team. We have also begun to look more deeply into servant-style leadership and a process for identifying the strengths of a congregation. From that vantage, we look at felt needs. At some point, a servant leader needs to work with the emerging renewal to establish an actual plan for renewal.

Some of the hardest and most creative work must now be done. By this time servant leaders have identified many talents and needs. People are gaining interest and may be willing to come forward and even be ready to serve. How do we put it all together?

Envisioning is the art of seeing things whole, as God would have them.[44] To make this vision become reality, we need to take small steps and work by stages. In Isaiah, the servant leaders feel a sense of call. The Servant is to lead the nation to be a light for others so that all can become the people of God. This doesn't happen overnight.

How can vision, strengths, and needs come together in a plan? The plan can have program and may involve some emphasis. Servant leaders are attuned to where God is calling and how things can work together to yield growth and renewal. We need to see the context in which new life can take form. With a vision, leaders try to identify the traits of the "baby" that is coming to birth (cf. John 1:12-13). With a plan, they make sure there are helpers and supplies on hand to nurture their renewed family of God.

A number of years ago, I was in a congregation where we identified the strengths of the Sunday school. There were many talented people. At the same time, there were many needs. We looked at both the talents and needs and clustered them together in groupings. We were able to create a tentative purpose statement.

However, we realized that not all needs could be met at once. As a group we began to weigh priorities. At the same time, we tried to decide which emphasis could build upon another emphasis. Some things logically came first; others would have to wait.

Some people were excited about certain programs and yet were willing to wait, knowing that they were going to happen at a specific date in the future. The people put a purpose statement on a large sheet of paper along with a time line. They listed a workshop, a time of taking pictures, a Bible study, and a program. On the time line, they placed them where they would appear in spring or fall in a three-year focus.

The associate pastor in this multiple-staff congregation found this process changing the people's mood from negative to positive. People were more ready to respond! Individuals became more deliberate about their calling and matching gifts to ministry opportunities in the congregation. As they did so, they were more willing to faithfully volunteer and accept these tasks. Staff reported that the mood of the congregation shifted from being afraid to being ready to try something new. They became eager to take some risks and to respond to new ministry opportunities.

Midway in the process, there was a review of progress. The church had established three small groups for fellowship and study. Two more groups were anticipated in the next year. The church had held a listening skills workshop for people in the Christian education department.

By this midpoint, all objectives except one were accomplished. The group felt it was best for the remaining objective not to be done by a committee. There was general excitement about what had happened. The church had moved from being reactive to being proactive.

That is one example of a renewal plan. Others can be given. The role of servant leaders is to listen intently to what is being said and to help the group focus on its mission and discover how it can be accomplished. In this instance, prioritizing was effective and helped each person feel included. By having a plan, the group was able to do one ministry at a time and have one build upon another. As time moves on, some new direction might emerge, and then the plan can be altered. A flexible plan helps us get moving.

A similar way of going about this process is to have the

group look at their biblical vision statement after they have identified their strengths and needs. In this process, it is also helpful to understand how this church nurtures people spiritually, so leaders can point activities in that direction.

There is a further advantage of using a Scripture. We can look at how the dynamics of faith in that passage speak to us. We saw how a passage like Revelation 7 could be used for insight into renewal (see chapter 3). As we delve into it more deeply, we discover more and more the dynamics of renewal and transformation in that context.

One could single out worship in Revelation 7:9-17 and work for renewal just around that theme. A servant leader with a renewal team may sense that the congregation could be renewed by beginning with worship. A three-year plan could be built to include such experiences as a study of the purpose of worship, seeing how worship is response to God, and perhaps studying the aspects of worship as found in Isaiah 6.[45]

Building on that, the church could have a workshop on singing. The saints adored God and sang the sevenfold doxology. All were involved—all 144,000 saints (Rev. 14:3). Not everyone is a singer, but everyone is in the chorus! Looking at the hymnal as a worship resource for six months can be a powerful tool for restoring the meaning of worship. Soloists and quartets can present special numbers. The prelude can be offered by a flutist and the postlude by someone playing a trumpet, especially if you are studying Revelation!

Everyone is part of this affirmation of God. The role of lay leadership can be explored and a worship team trained. Worship leaders can conduct a portion of the service, and the pastor can sit with the congregation. Gifts of young and old can be utilized as part of the service.

Certainly a preaching emphasis could be pursued. Servant leaders can explore the shift in preaching when we move from preaching at people (which no one likes) to speaking the word with people. The listening style of the servant leader can be incorporated into the partnering style suggested by James Forbes.[46] The preacher pauses to listen to responses from the congregation, and takes time to process questions they raise. Others in the congregation may also offer words of exhortation.

Renewed worship can become a vital part of a renewal plan. Exploring key biblical texts can be instrumental in building a renewal plan. The role of leadership is to help the renewal team with the decision of how the congregation can be helped in growing spiritually and how needs can be met and talents utilized. Servant leaders look at how the vision can be fulfilled. Certainly there is nothing more effective in renewal than to have a revitalization of worship.

A leader can help the renewal team utilize a biblical text and see how all of the dynamics of renewal can become part of a renewal plan. Looking at our passage in Revelation, one can consider how each of the four components of the text can build on one another. One stage of renewal can be in worship, as already mentioned. Another stage can be that of transformation.

Wouldn't it be exciting to have a six-month emphasis on how people's lives are changed by their faith in God? Classes of all ages could discuss such a study. Since the congregation has been sharing how their faith has been formed, the servant leader can encourage the telling of such stories more widely. This can be done through the newsletter, in the church school, or in the Sunday worship. Faith formation can become a much more central part of the church's life.

Roy Oswald of the Alban Institute led our pastors' conference for the Church of the Brethren in South Carolina in 1995. He shared how few pastors have been trained in the vital area of leading people through the experience of transformation in faith.[47] While faith transformation is at the heart of the church's ministry, we have been rather sparse in our discussion of such a topic. We need to focus on this area of our life as a congregation, and we can do so through preaching, teaching, and sharing.

What if a whole church discussed how their lives had been changed in faith, not just as a once-and-for-all experience but as a continual deepening through various experiences in their lives? How rich such sharing can be in small groups, in adult and teen and children's classes, and in fellowship times! Here people can share the positive experiences of feeling God's grace and love at important times and ordinary times in life. What a way to renew the church!

After worship and faith transformation, we can continue with the dynamics of renewal from the passage in Revelation. What if we looked at the Lamb who became the Shepherd and examined the whole servant-leader focus in Revelation 7? For years I have been sharing with classes of pastors about holding servant-leader or in-service training throughout the church.

On their jobs, many people have such regular training. What about servant-style leadership training for trustees, deacons, stewards, Christian education departments, the pastoral board, and all the rest of the organization? The entire church could become aware of the servant style and learn concrete leadership skills (see worksheet 6). The time would be well spent. Servant-leader training and spiritual renewal would be likely results.

Finally, Revelation 7 also focuses on the dynamic of drinking from the fountains of living water. What an imagery to draw from! Recent renewal worship services have used actual fountains of one kind or another for a worship center. One church I attended had a flowing fountain as a symbolic part of the sanctuary.

What if a whole church began to share, not only how they have been refreshed by the Living Water, but also how they can use their gifts daily in ministry to others? Churches can go on to see how servant-oriented evangelism can become a vital part of their ministry.[48] A current model for such servant-style faith sharing is doing random acts of kindness, things that witness to one's faith.[49]

Using a biblical text, the servant leader needs to help the renewal team and congregation see how the dynamics of renewal can result in some plan of ministry. Servant leaders help the team envision the future and represent that vision in a diagram or outline.

On servant leadership, Robert Greenleaf speaks about conceptualizing as the prime leadership talent. Greenleaf gives the example of Nikolai Frederik Severin Grundtvig, the father of the Danish folk high school. Many reforms had been made for the sake of the peasants, but none *by* them. Grundtvig, a theologian, visited with the common people. After listening, he responded to their aspirations by conceptualizing a school where young adults could learn about Danish history and poetry.

After high schools were established and peasant youths were being educated there, they also began to attend agricultural schools and build cooperatives. These developments transformed Danish culture and sustained it even through wartime.

Grundtvig himself never operated a folk high school. However, his love for the poor and his clear vision and deep dedication led him to share his faith with them. Their spirits were roused to meet the challenge of the day.[50]

In a similar manner, the servant leader can help a renewal committee facilitate a congregation's renewal. To build a plan of renewal, leaders need to conceptualize what is possible. To do that, they have to step back in prayer, pause in silence, listen, and discern God's Spirit and movement.

The servant leader sees that, rather than doing this process alone, the renewal team and others can be a vital part of the process. Members of a renewal team will grow closer as they pray together, discuss together, and then work together to see a renewal plan unfold. This is hard work, but what a blessing to be part of it!

Anticipating, Initiating, Timing

Anticipating, initiating, and timing are three essential aspects of organizing. Bypassing one can seriously limit any of the organizing one might do.

Anticipating means prayerfully looking at all the factors on the horizon and intuitively and prayerfully sensing what should happen to help vision become reality.

Initiating means saying in effect, "Let's go."

Timing means sensing the right time to get started and the right time to take a breather.

All three of these factors must be considered by the servant leader.

Jesus, the Servant of all, was a Master at all three traits of good leadership. When he was anticipating his Last Supper with his disciples and the impending events, he illustrated his servanthood by washing his disciples' feet (John 13). His drama of servanthood was enacted at the right moment to instruct his disciples. The Master held to his vision and demonstrated it creatively by producing a drama proclaiming his message.

In a similar manner, Jesus initiated leadership when he called Zacchaeus down from the tree and told him that he was going to come eat at his house that day (Luke 19). Jesus was a master of timing, as shown when the Jewish leaders caught the woman in adultery (John 8). He quietly drew in the sand and then made his statement. Jesus knew when the right hour had come.

Servant leaders anticipate what is to come, initiate renewal, and time responses for the right moment. For example, a renewal team knows plans are best started in the fall or spring, though there certainly will be exceptions, depending on one's vision. If a plan is to be activated in the fall of the year, initiative must be taken in the prior spring to get everything in place. Anticipation and timing are crucial.

If your winters are too harsh to have regular night meetings, you may be restricted to Lent or even after Easter. If your church is busy during Lent, hold smaller, behind-the-scenes preparatory meetings during Lent and any needed congregational meetings after Easter. Anyhow, the Easter season till Pentecost is the historic time for renewal in the church. However, such meetings should take place before graduation and summer activities. In May, enlist the help of people for the fall. Make last-minute plans in June. Enter September with renewal plans ready to go!

Initiating is one aspect of leadership that needs attention. You may ask, "How does one initiate as a servant leader without knowing whether the renewal plan is on target well enough or will have the right results?"

I tell church leaders that if nothing is done, nothing will happen. It is better to begin somewhere and then to make adjustments. While initiatives might not be totally on target, let us be flexible enough to change and to do it another way the next time.

Servant leaders must also be aware that renewal comes in unexpected moments that cannot be planned. Sometimes it is out of such experiences that a vision for renewal can be sharpened or even take on a whole new direction. What happens is because initiative, based on that inner leading of God's Spirit, was taken.

As a result of careful and prayerful anticipating and organizing, congregational members will mention how on target a ministry is. They may ask, "How did you know what was so needed?" The hard work of organizing for renewal and then of anticipating the right approach, initiating what is needed, and doing it when the timing is right— all these steps help things unfold naturally.

The sense of "rightness" is a testimony to the spiritual groundwork that was laid in prayer and organizing. As a result people are nurtured spiritually. In addition, they sense a shared investment as well as a shared reward.

An example of all this is a well-received family night

ministry at the Mohler congregation, during my service as interim pastor. An evening children's program came to a grinding halt due to old misunderstandings. Rising out of the ashes of conflict (cf. Esther 4:1-3), I spent time in prayer. I sensed that some type of program should be put in place to build on the strengths of the church and to meet the needs of the congregation. Healing can't take place in a vacuum.

Therefore, we designed a family night built on the youth club concept, where every child has a sponsor who helps make the program possible.[51] There would be a meal, singing, classes for all ages, and a service project. The service project would be knotting comforters that the older aid circle in the church made for relief.

This built on strengths of the church: cooking, commitment of sponsors, and a service orientation. With just 140-150 in worship services, we averaged 100-110 in the first quarter of the family night program. Even before our renewal plan was set in place by our envisioning committee, this first building block was a bridge into the future.

Implementing Renewal Ministries

It may seem premature to speak about implementing ministries in a chapter on organizing for renewal. But implementing plans for renewal already begins as the first thought or plan is made. With the very spirit of such an effort comes the first movement toward accomplishment. What the servant leader understands is that all the inner work is exemplified externally as renewal begins.

Hence, we can and should talk about carrying out ministries so we don't make such a difference between organizing and implementing. Besides, it is the implementation that takes the most effort. If the organizing includes getting started practically, then things have a better chance for success.

A leader's function in carrying out renewal is very important. One aspect of implementation is ensuring that proper training is available. After we discern talents and enlist people, we need to provide training so they have the skills and resources to do a ministry.

Training is more than offering know-how. It is vital to a person's development in faith. Taking up any ministry is potentially formative in a person's life. Why not offer supportive training that brings out the real skills of people and helps them feel confident in what they are doing?

Servant leaders are sensitive about getting such training done in a style that builds on people's strengths and helps meet their needs and needs of those to whom they minister. One outstanding example of this developed at the Bush Creek Church, where I did the doctor of ministry training.

The church held extensive teacher training sessions and conducted a supervision unit for youth counselors. It also developed an active adult education elective class that increased in attendance from six to an average of forty-four people. Both new people and old resident members were interested in the foundations of biblical studies as well as classes on the church's beliefs. They also appreciated regular courses on family life, current concerns, and practical life issues.

We designed a series of courses taught on a twelve-to-fifteen-week rotation year-round. We obtained resources for each course and enlisted teams of teachers, often with an experienced teacher and someone else with teaching gifts but little or no experience.

As pastor, I would sit down with the team well ahead of the course and help the teachers design their classes and gather needed resources. Since I knew what helps they were going to use in teaching, I often carried those resources around in my car and shared them with potential class members. Many people learned what foundations in faith were necessary to help with teaching in the church. A lot of teachers were trained in the process.

For others, the adult elective class became a healthy

haven for people who wanted to take a rest from other responsibilities. Many cherished being in the class for a quarter, in an active and alive adult teaching-learning situation. In terms of organizing for renewal, it was an excellent way to develop a pool of potential leaders.

Any new leaders who are taking up a new ministry on a regular basis will need some supervision. A mentor can be available to check in with any person who is taking up a new ministry on a regular basis.[52] In terms of organizing for renewal, it is valuable to have some procedure in place so that new people in ministry can be served in this way.

The Elizabethtown Church of the Brethren, to which we referred earlier, developed a whole system of mentoring for new teachers. Since the renewal team has so many tasks, other committees (such as a nominating committee or a gifts discernment committee) may be helpful for leadership development. Rather than getting people to fill slots, we carefully assess people, their gifts, and the development of their ministries. Training is a key component in implementing a renewal plan.

Another area of organizing for renewal is encouraging renewal. One of the best ways to enhance renewal is to encourage people's efforts, confirm the new life that is happening, and show appreciation for the gifts each person offers. Such encouragement can come in informal short notes or in more formal certificates. It can mean more than ever imagined! Being in homes in the city, I have often seen certificates of appreciation framed and hanging on the walls in people's homes years later. Servant leaders can facilitate such opportunities on a regular and natural basis.

Getting organized is a crucial part of the renewal process. Led by the Spirit of God, servant leaders can help organize in a way that models the very growth envisioned. Each effort can be part of the whole. Leaders can value and affirm others, encourage them to use their gifts, and help them get their needs met along the way. Drawing forth people's talents can be an exciting endeavor in training, in supervising, and in encouraging. However, a leader's tasks are not complete without looking at some other key areas. What hardships might be encountered? How do servant leaders continue for the long haul in renewal? How do they help the church become a more serving community? Furthermore, how does leadership renew and celebrate?

We will explore these questions in chapters 7 and 8. Let us first look at how servant leaders help an entire church become a more serving community.

6
Servant Leadership and Servant Structures

While writing this book, my family and I traveled, in a venture of faith, to Perryville, Arkansas. Our younger son was to be part of a youth work camp at the Heifer Project ranch. The more I became involved in the work camp and learned about the organization, the more I realized how God was on this journey—and on the journey of Heifer Project International.

The Heifer Project International (HPI) is an organization that just marked its fiftieth anniversary. It is headquartered in Little Rock, totally driven by faith, and living in service. HPI had a lot to teach me about servant leadership and servant structures. With its permission, I began to study its leadership style and structures so I could share them with you here. HPI is indeed a vibrant servant structure.

It is crucial for renewal to have the right kinds of structures to foster the mission and vision to which the church feels called. Structures are more than meetings and committees. They are all the ways in which we operate. They do not need to be dull and lifeless; they can be creative and life-giving.

Structures are organization, both formal and informal, but they are also more. They include lines of communication, lines of accountability, and lines of delegation to carry out decisions. Training is part of structure. Taking care of one another involves structure. Part of the role of structures is to offer evaluation and appreciation. Learning about structures is important.

Born of a vision, Heifer Project was begun when a Church of the Brethren man, Dan West, went to Spain to give out powdered milk after the Spanish Civil War. Dan began to realize that a cup of milk helps to feed a child for a day, but a cow would give milk for a lifetime. Dan returned home to Indiana and presented the idea to his church. Virgil Mock said, "Have Faith, Dan West," according to the new children's book on the project. [53] Dan responded, "I have faith, but I need a cow." Virgil Mock explained that *Faith* was the name of the Guernsey cow he was giving Dan. It was the first of three cows named Faith, Hope, and Charity. Thus Heifer Project International was born.

There is a simplicity to Dan's dream that has now extended to 120 countries in the world. Five regional offices span the United States to help churches and civic organizations contribute to "not a cup but a cow." The program is a simple plan: people who receive a cow give the first female offspring to another family. The recipients are then not just receiving but are becoming part of the giving chain.

Before Heifer Project gives someone a cow, it establishes a training program in animal care and ensures proper preparation of the animal's quarters. At present, more than heifers are given. Goats, sheep, chickens, and even fish are donated to those in need. [54]

Heifer Project International has a well-worked-out statement of purpose, vision, and mission:

> In response to God's love for all people, the mission of HPI is, in partnership with others, to alleviate hunger, poverty, and environmental degradation by—
> A. Responding to requests for development assistance, including animals, training, and technical assistance, which enables families to seek self-reliance in food production and income generation on a sustainable basis.

B. Enabling people to share ("pass on the gift") in a way that enhances dignity and offers everyone the opportunity to make a difference in the struggle to alleviate hunger and poverty.

C. Educating people about the root causes of hunger and poverty, based on HPI's experience and insight gained from working with animals in development projects since 1944.

D. Supporting people in sustainable development and the stewardship of the environment through responsible management of animal resources.[55]

Praying for the Structures One by One

Returning again to our prayer life, servant leaders best begin by praying through the church structures. They consider in prayer each aspect of the congregation's organization, how each assigned task can become a living part of the vision, and how all these projects can better serve the needs of individuals and of the church body. Structures quickly start operating. Leaders' prayer life can help structures be shaped to serve people in a Christian, compassionate way.

Leadership can help in this process of stepping back and focusing. The pause to focus can help leaders be creative in thinking and gain the energy for the daily task.

Developing servant structures means to form an organization that embodies the church's mission, serving the need for which it is established. With serving structures, we serve God, and in so doing learn to serve others. To do that, the servant "kneels into structures." What does that mean?

I recall a blessed aspect of spending a week in a work camp at the Heifer Project International ranch. We had the opportunity to sit in on the Wednesday morning (7:15 a.m.) Bible study for all staff and volunteers. The fellowship was enriching; the Bible study was creative and uplifting. The group was studying Proverbs and wondering what they would find in it that could apply to their work.

They came onto Proverbs 14:4 and concluded that it is a great verse for HPI: "Where no oxen are, the crib is clean; but much increase is by the strength of the ox" (KJV). The challenge the owner of the oxen faced was whether to go to the trouble of having an ox. After all, the ox eats some of the very grain the farmer is hoping to produce.

However, without the ox and its cost, "the barn is empty" (NEB), the cupboard is bare. The ox is needed to help produce crops: "Where there are no oxen, there is no grain; abundant crops come by the strength of the ox" (NRSV).

Those who have wisdom, however, see beyond the immediate mess, trouble, and hardship of work and keep the goal in view (cf. 2 Thess. 3:10). One person observed that in scouting organizations, the den mothers doing the best job seemed to have the messiest homes! Many chuckled at that thought.

Our prayers that day were deeper. We realized that a lot of prayerful energy goes into all that an organization (such as HPI) produces, and into each task along the way, even as a lot of mess is created. Wisdom, that deeper discernment of God, revealed to us that such times for meditation and prayer are valuable, and the structures created are important.

How much more important it is that we pray through our structures in the church so that they are expressions of our faith, our vision, and our service! In a closing prayer after the Bible study, a woman powerfully summarized this statement of faith: "Make me a servant, humble and meek."

Now keeping all this practical, we are faced in the church with how to keep structures serving the purpose God has assigned to us. We want structures serving need and structures being ministry.

In the church renewal plan at Bush Creek, we faced the whole question as leadership used a structure that was old and large. Would we use an existing organizational pattern that needed fifty to sixty people to work? Or would we go to a more-streamlined organization, using perhaps twenty? We were helped by having a vision statement that guided our purpose. Our plan of renewal followed a focus statement: "To enable the Bush Creek Church to discover Christ's calling and so to lead to greater commitment in faith and greater love for persons."

On the time line, to be completed in two and a half years, we had further vision statements: "motivation for the congregation from faith in Christ," "tapping the variety of resources," "let all feel a part," "a larger base of active members with responsibility spread to many," "an organ that pulls together and gives focus for where the church is called."

It was a real faith experience to have a viable structure as a church that included people and helped them grow in their ministry.

We began a plan of renewal with baby steps. The first was just to have board meetings be regular and for a real purpose. We needed to see that people were being heard. We also needed to see that we were getting somewhere, implementing decisions, being held accountable, increasing the level of congregational interest, and effectively focusing our efforts.

Each of these subgoals went with revitalizing the board. For this old system to work, the chair really had to represent the commission at the board meetings. Each commission chair needed to carry back information and decisions of the board to the commissions.[56]

First we put the focus and vision and purpose statements together. Then it was easy to answer whether or not to reorganize or attempt to get the existing organization up and running again. Being part of a commission, if it were alive in faith and accomplishing its purpose, could be a real faith experience.

With new people coming into the church, sharing the

load meant tapping new resources and spreading responsi-bility. Reorganizing always takes a lot of effort. We saw the needs of people and of organization for stability and conti-nuity. Thus it seemed wise and prudent to reactivate the old structure rather than create a totally new one. Many indi-viduals could learn how they could serve.

Having a viable organization could actually be a faith experience. A lot of what we call assimilating occurred in the process as people met and worked on committees with people they otherwise would never have known.

In this way, the leaders kept their vision in focus. They stayed rooted in faith, tapped available resources, spread out responsibility, and pulled together.

Likewise, in other churches servant leaders also keep guiding the renewal of faith, and everything moves toward vision. This means they keep spiritually focused. They also meet with committee chairs to prepare agendas, initiate a training sessions in servant leadership, and encourage peo-ple in implementing ministries.

Other times, servant leaders see how tasks can be coor-dinated so that a truly living and vibrant church body is formed. Such organizations, when prayed through, become more open structures and more creative, including new people. A lot of hard work goes into serving through an organization.

Beginning this process by centering in prayer is not time wasted. It is crucial to pause before asking for God's guid-ing vision and looking at the resources available before plunging into the work. We saw real evidence of this at Heifer Project International. It all began in prayer. Soon we saw how all worked together, staff and volunteers. A com-mon spirit was evident; a focus was present.

Hence, as we begin to create servant structures, let us pause first to pray so that we gain a workable vision. This means following God's leading, using the strengths of the situation, and having the spiritual sensitivity to begin this endeavor. Regular prayer at a meeting can become more than a ceremonial add-on. It can be a vital part of discerning God's direction and gaining the strength to do the labors.

Creating a Team

While at the Heifer Project work camp, I had my first real introduction to a ropes course. The director of training took me out to the site where groups learn how to become a team. People in the groups ranged from school children to senior executives.

In the course was a series of wood blocks. The whole group had to learn how to put a series of boards over the stationary parts so they could traverse between them. The instructor explained that each individual was needed to do their part. Often someone who doesn't often shine would end up being a key player by figuring out the puzzle.

Through the week at the Heifer ranch, we were learning how to be a team. In one exercise, the leader asked the group to join hands in a circle, with a Hula Hoop hanging on one pair of arms. Then the hoop was passed over one head and down over one pair of legs without breaking the chain. They passed the hoop around the ring, person by person. Each one helped the next through. When finished, the group proclaimed, "We did it."

Next, two people go through the hoop at the same time, again without breaking the chain. It takes more teamwork by the group to accomplish this.

Then three people work their way through the hoop at the same time. The game goes on until the limit is reached. This exercise builds a good sense of teamwork and feeling of accomplishment.

As a church, we need to work at creating teams. When a group takes on a task, the people need to discuss how to do the work cooperatively. Otherwise, one person may feel left to do everything. On the other hand, if one is energetic and does it all, then the rest feel left out by default. It takes effort to identify the skills and availability of each member. However, this work is what creates a group spirit. "We did it!" can be a corporate expression of true accomplishment. The hoop game can be used to help create this kind of cooperative spirit. I brought back the hoops exercises to use at our church picnic, and it proved both fun and instructive.

Servant leaders learn a style of teamwork. In this, they see that they are modeling the church. Each person's gifts are being used. The servant leader is working with individuals in the congregation. The leader offers a word of encouragement as needed. Rather than just taking on a task, the servant leader looks at how the talents of others can be used and developed. The expression becomes "we" rather than "I." All of this can be preventative medicine to ward off burnout that can come even through good intentions. Servants learn to think "team."

We have already seen what happened at the Elizabethtown Church in terms of inner spiritual renewal and the youth ministry council. The behind-the-scenes story is just as important. Integral to the success of this story was the planning by the envisioning committee. They were created to help envision the future of the congregation.

The committee looked at the three movements of spiritual growth and the seven-stage process of renewal. Then they took off with the idea of getting as many people involved in Lenten groups as possible. That happened consistently as they identified and utilized a variety of leaders for anything from leading worship to leading discussion groups. Their whole emphasis was on joining together in spiritual growth.

No wonder an outgrowth of this was a youth ministry council! When the call came to form a mission statement, the envisioning committee asked the youths to go to their respective classes to receive input on their mission. At our second meeting of the youth ministry council, we invited each to share about significant memories from their own youth. Many reported how their faith had been formed.

The impact of this whole endeavor has been so great that the adults asked, "What about us?" So an adult ministry council has been put on the drawing boards. A year later I hear interest coming together to get that started. Teamwork fosters teamwork.

In church-leader circles, there is talk of "systems improvement." Out of the family systems approach, we are learning a lot about healthy families of God. As teams are formed, we can develop and nurture healthy relationships. In systems theory, we examine interactions. We look at the whole to explain the parts, rather than analyzing just the parts to explain the whole.

Factors that keep things the same are *homeostatic*. They preserve *homeostasis* or equilibrium. Usually a system gets up and operating in a certain way. However, homeostasis can keep things from changing and can actually be counter-productive.[57] When change is proposed, we often hear the old way defended simply because it came first: "But that's the way we've always done things." Such homeostasis at work might block the "new thing" the Lord wants to do (Isa. 43:19).

So much is being written about codependency and relationships that are unhealthy. By utilizing spiritual resources, healthy relationships can be developed. Praying through structures can keep systems responsive to needs.

Creating teams to be serving structures is key to this development. God calls us to develop systems and structures that serve need and uplift individuals. Structures that are merely self-serving and self-perpetuating will not satisfy. If leaders create teams that are meeting the needs of others, then teamwork is occurring.

Such teams are a model and expression of the ministry being performed. They can be anything from a men's prayer group to a soup kitchen or a bereavement support group. It takes a lot of hard work—and maybe some messes—to form such ministries.

However, ministries like these ring true to the gospel, which calls us to feed the hungry, clothe the naked, console the afflicted, and encourage the fainthearted (Matt. 25:31-36; 2 Cor. 1:4; Gal. 6:1-2, 10). The church's authenticity will speak loudly. What begins with prayer is lived out in ministries of service.

Such teams speak the very message they are called to implement. In the process of serving this way, we grow in faith.

Working as a Team

Not only do we want to form effective teams; we want to continue to work as effective teams. At the Heifer Project ranch, I saw how important this was to the workers. The head gardener made sure he gave good orientation and directions. The gardener explained the purpose behind what we were doing and how to do it.

In this case, we were actually making an organic garden. We learned how this could help ecologically; we also were taught proper techniques of preparing the soil. We used giant sifters to get rid of rocks. By so doing, we created mounds of dirt. On top of the dirt, we put mulch to retain moisture. Each person had a job to do.

In the process, I noticed how people's needs were cared for. The gardener encouraged everyone to drink regularly so no one would suffer adverse effects from the scorching heat. A container of water was provided under a nearby tree.

The manner of encouragement from the gardener was important. He would say that it was not just the product that was important, but how one was doing in the process of accomplishing it. The whole process was very person centered as well as product oriented. The balance of the two was strongly evident. It is crucial for servant leaders to keep the needs of people in mind while building a program. So often this is the downfall of a renewal movement. It can be the downfall of a church when it moves from a pastor-sized church to a program-sized church. So often programs or results are valued above the people being served. In that case, the balance of people and program is easily lost.

In a marvelous little booklet that keeps us focused, *The Life Cycle of the Congregation,* Martin Saarinen looks at the life cycle of a congregation. With his bell curve of growth and decline, Saarinen tracks four "genes" of growth: energy, program, administration, and inclusion. He labels each component of a congregation with a letter, small or large, to indicate where that gene is dominant or fading into the background. In growth, the p factor for program becomes more dominant in the upswing, and the i factor for inclusion is overridden.

Saarinen says, "The intentionality of the congregation tends to become more focused on the requirement of programs and services at the expense of people needs; hence the diminished "I."[58] For maturing to occur, *both* the program factor and inclusion factor must be kept in balance.

In building servant structures, servant leaders need to monitor carefully the effect of decisions on people. What people does this decision cut out of the program and potentially out of the body? To put it positively, how can we draw people in while at the same time establishing clearly defined programs? How can the vision of our structure not only draw people in and include them but also build upon their gifts?

Servant leadership monitors, works, intervenes, reminds, helps envision, and calls forth others' gifts. In this way, people's needs are not neglected but rather are served. This care for people needs to happen while leaders are building structures to serve a growing congregation. In other words, let us draw people in rather than leave them out when building the body of Christ. We call it assimilation, not just of new people but also of talented, long-term leaders. They all make up Christ's church. How do we do that? There are only so many days in the week. There are only so many hours of the day. Whatever way we make a decision, we cause schedule conflicts.

Before we go down any road of program development, we must slow down to consult with people—the very pool of people whose talents we envision using and the people we hope to serve. Even though this takes longer, in the long run it can be a real time-saver. If we have to reverse direction, that consumes a lot of energy—the energy of leaders and ultimately the energy of those to be served.

In establishing a program, let us first ask, How will this program include people—those being served, those finding fulfillment through offering their talents, and those who might be new? How do we make this idea accessible to all? How do we foster an atmosphere in which people can grow? How are people growing in faith? How are people doing personally along the way? How are they experiencing the love of the body of Christ? How are "the least of these" treated as the work is promoted?

Funding Servant Structures

Crucial in creating servant structures is funding them. We may think that servant leaders should not have to worry about such mundane matters. However, integral to the work of a team is having the necessary ingredients. Funds are just as important as ideas! Especially as a plan of ministry is formulated, part of making the plan practical is to have funds in place to provide for the program.

While at the Heifer Project ranch, I had a chance to interview people integrally involved in funding. The regional office on the ranch is consistently running in the black despite being located in a poor area of Arkansas. So I asked for the key to their financial success. In response, the coordinator said it all boiled down to one key word: *believability*. At first I thought she meant getting me to believe in her program, but that was not it. She meant that *she* was believing in their own undertaking. The coordinator radiated enthusiasm that inspired others. She also did a lot of hard work, such as sending follow-up and thank-you notes. Her belief in the organization and commitment to it was convincingly apparent.

People can sense a certain positive spirit in a serving organization. They can quickly tell when needs are being met. That is why so many give to projects. They can see specific results, particular needs being met. In raising funds for any organization, one must help potential givers see how the targeted needs are being met.

Even in unified giving with a combined budget, people want to know that their money is going to the proper place. They have heard of enough deception and disappointment. When an organization is meeting needs and changing lives, contributors feel that they are effective partners in mission. Then people can relate real-life stories of what is happening. Effective funding of a church is usually a clear indicator of the spirit of the whole congregation.

What we are looking for is good stewardship.[59] A "steward" is someone put in charge of something for somebody else. A steward is called to administer or put in order the household of another. Sometimes called servants, stewards are responsible for even more than money. They are to protect and maintain the householder's building and its general welfare.

In the New Testament, the meaning of *steward* expands to include care and compassion. Jesus talks about the Good Shepherd, who does not run away like the hired hand (John 10). As followers of Christ, it is crucial for us to give care.

The steward has unconditional love for what is entrusted to him.[60]

Servant leaders understand that stewardship applies to all of life. The servant is a steward, and the steward is a servant. As servants, stewards see that they are merely caretakers of another's property. They are not building their own fiefdom. A steward will foster a better sense of respect that builds trust.

That is why such seemingly small things like thank-you notes, genuinely written and delivered, are so important in the renewal process. People begin to sense a commitment and a spirit that speaks of unconditional love. Stewardship has trust at its heart. Trust is at the heart of building a budget in any organization, especially those that operate on goodwill.

The feeling that someone is serving another builds trust. When people observe that a leader is doing something not for self-aggrandizement but for the good of others, they respond from the heart, often generously.

People can be enlisted in their wish to be servants themselves. If giving can help people fulfill their own goals, then asking for help is really part of serving them, since they desire to be of service.

Thank-you messages can convey how the project has been going, like a progress report. It is much easier to build servant structures when a high level of appreciation and trust are at work. Servant leaders understand and have a sense of reverence around the whole process of giving. Thus fundraising is not an appendix. Instead, it is an integral part of the entire mission. A servant is marked as a servant insofar as the spirit of funding is understood and carried out.

Servant leaders have a special view of their undertaking. Rather than pushing their product on others, they help others discover the joy of giving to something worthy. Servant leaders come alongside people and help them accomplish their goals. They influence potential supporters through listening, encouraging, and persuading rather than through high-pressure sales tactics.

How we approach fundraising is so important. It signals whether we are helping people fulfill a shared ministry or whether we want just their money. Individuals soon understand the message we are sending. Our goal is to serve people even as they are sharing and serving with their hard-earned substance.

7

Servant Leadership and Handling Hardship

When we were at the Heifer Project ranch, one of the giant water buffalo broke his nose ring, got untied, and gored the other water buffalo. It was a hot day, and apparently one buffalo became a little unnerved. The whole area was thrown into pandemonium. Everyone was afraid of what might happen next.

Happily, the trainer was able to break up the fight and bring back some order. I asked him how he did it. He replied that, though the beasts were frightening, he had developed rapport with the water buffalo by taking them down to the watering hole every day. Through his relationship with them, he was able to command them, "Stop." And they responded.

This story offers some helpful pointers for servant leaders facing hardship and conflict. All servant leaders have to face some form of difficulty sooner or later. The experience will be trying. That is the time to hold up vision, set clear boundaries, build on relationships already developed, and attempt to grow deeper.

Servant leaders know in their hearts that this is a difficult time for all. So they slow the pace a bit and take time to listen, reassess, and hold firm. Servant leaders know it is time to listen to the movement of God, who is at work even through difficulty. The trainer of the water buffalo knew the parameters in which to operate. Human relationships need such boundaries as well.

Being in Hardship

Hardship tests one's mettle. We may wonder whether we have what it takes. How do we handle fear and feelings of inadequacy? During such a time, it is helpful to review the traits of the Servant leader, as given in the Servant Songs of Isaiah (see chapter 1, above).

The Servant has no form or beauty. Just having a better appearance or better equipment or more sophisticated theology is not going to make difficulty go away. It is amazing that transformation has little to do with outward form. Instead, what is crucial is inward motivation and perspective. According to the Servant Songs, the Lord God will help the Servant fulfill the assigned mission.

We came to the Mohler Church of the Brethren while they were in the midst of discouragement. The Mohler Church is smaller than the Elizabethtown Church, earlier cited as an example. The Mohler church has about 140 people in attendance and is somewhere between a pastor-sized and a program-sized church.

Until recently, Mohler did not have a paid pastor. Its membership strikes one as having their roots in country life, with suburbia growing up around them. In terms of leadership, Mohler felt inadequate, although quite open to leadership training. Like Elizabethtown, it is a church that is open to renewal and cares deeply for people. Both congregations have a very strong faith heritage.

When I entered the congregation as interim pastor, it was a time to evaluate, increase communication, and gain stability. People sensed a need for a renewal and wanted to grow deeper in faith.

By being servants and rubbing shoulders with people who are servants, we find that it is not the appearance that transforms, but rather the quality of the servant's life. Without even knowing it, servant leaders who follow their vision and embody faithfulness can have a tremendous impact on others. Their sincerity speaks; their loving service to others carries a powerful message. In times of difficulty and uncertainty, they can call upon others to augment a team. Perhaps unnoticed at first, the servant leader can speak a message that ultimately makes a tremendous impact.

For the book *In Search of Excellence,* Thomas Peters and Robert Waterman did major research on high-performance companies. They discovered that companies moving toward excellence had corporate goals to which employees were committed. Their approach always had two traits: they valued their customers, and they valued their employees.

At first the researchers did not think this had anything to do with developing anything other than ordinary individuals, but continued research found otherwise. They found that early in the successful company's existence, there were one or two individuals who were really committed to corporate goals and values. There is a false sense of security if individuals merely hold onto their jobs but are not truly committed to the goals and values of the company. Transforming leadership raises people to a higher plain of purpose and action, thereby raising motivation and values.[61]

In the church, having servant leaders who are transformed by Christ is fundamental to developing a healthy organism. In time of hardship, it is just as important to be as to do. Servant leaders learn that simply being present can be extremely important. A person's knees may shake during the crisis, like the trainer of the water buffalo. It is natural to react or become upset. But servant leaders learn that this is when they need to draw on their God-given inner strength.

The Servant Songs remind us that God will give the servants the needed strength. Having seen difficulty themselves, they know that times of hardship can also bring growth. The quality of one's inner life with God can be sustaining. It is important to maintain both a sense of personal direction and a sense of group direction. Sometimes it is enough simply to be still and wait, on purpose (Isa. 40:31). "They also serve who only stand and wait" (Milton, "On His Blindness").

As the Mohler Church began to make great strides (related below), another period of discouragement came. The church again needed to pause and reflect. This time the future did not seem to be as formidable. Since we had come through some stages of renewal, we gained confidence from that experience and believed that we could continue.

I decided to take a whole day for a guided retreat, focusing on Moses and the burning bush. Again I was reminded how God came to Moses and called him. Even amid his objections, Moses gained a sense that the Lord would go with him. The focus of his activity would take him right back into life and leadership responsibilities. There was purpose and direction.

The retreat renewed me. I noticed in myself fresh energy, peacefulness, and quietness. In hardship, the servant leader learns to nourish inner peacefulness and to bring that to the situation at hand. Servant leaders then call people together as a team around vision.

Sustaining the Vision

Hardship may serve to reinforce our vision. From the Servant Songs, we remember how the Servant leader holds up vision for the people to be God's servants. Perhaps no more singular a trait can help a church move through hardship than for its people to remember their identity.

Servants leaders have a call. Servants leaders have a purpose. Servant leaders have a direction. When a church becomes discouraged, members find it difficult to know who they are. Servants leaders are to help the body be a light to the nations. They have a purpose to fulfill.

When everything is pulling apart, servant leaders have the unique ability to see things whole. Given their traits of listening and having a sense of God's leading, servant leaders can conceptualize how to translate vision into workable reality. This is establishing a measurable vision of what is possible, not unreachable goals.

Even in difficulty, servant leaders have an ability to see how things can fit together to move toward wholeness. Servant leaders work for what is possible and edifying. In hardship, they know it is essential to lift up the big picture.

At the Mohler Church of the Brethren, we eventually formed an envisioning committee during a time of uncertainty. I did not know whether a committee could choose a theme and go to work in such an atmosphere. However, not having a sense of direction was even more deadening.

Was it premature to attempt to plan for the future? In the middle of this dilemma, I shared with the district executive that it seemed like we needed to move forward.

He compared our situation with having a broken bone. After the bone is set, the patient has to begin exercising. So we began to set a direction. The board wanted to have a program for children. They said the problem was that we had few trained leaders. So we established important teacher training, to build up the Sunday school and any other program.

Our meetings seemed to help the board move into the future. With the approval of the board, I called together a set of leaders to form an envisioning committee, to begin the process of helping the church set a direction. This would give the people a sense that something positive was being put into place.

Churches often go through periods of just lumbering along without feeling like they are getting anywhere. They can sense that there is a problem, or they may know that certain real problems do exist. Unless and until people share their wounds and the air is cleared, fatigue sets in. In times of uncertainty, there is a loss of momentum. God may be nudging us to evaluate our situation and to foresee the future.

It may seem risky to try to solve problems. Nevertheless, as a pastor I have learned that it is actually riskier to let things go unattended. Proper boundaries need to be established. Trust must be carefully built up. People must be safeguarded from further hurt. Assistance must be offered to anyone who needs extra support as the church moves through stages of growth.

For renewal to occur, healing must begin. In fact, as a renewal process is set up, it becomes part of the healing.

The children's club at Mohler needed new focus. As this happened, people learned to pitch in and take part. Soon they decided to set up a program that would involve the entire family. They adopted the Youth Club International fourfold format, featuring a light meal and cooperative games, singing, study time, and a service project.

In our adaptation, this club was set up as an intergenerational event, for all ages. We maintained the stipulation that every child needs a sponsor or mentor, someone who would help with the program and give added support to each youngster during the months the club was running.[62] The congregation decided to adopt this emphasis for the Lenten season.

As the pastor, I had begun to offer specific challenges leading toward our vision. I did this about once a quarter for the entire congregation. This seemed to help us get up and moving. In this series, I challenged the congregation to host a family night for the entire church. This proposal was suitable because we sensed that there was a need for the church to do something positive, build healthy relationships, and grow spiritually.

As I anticipated, this family night had a great impact on the children, youth, and adults. Furthermore, having a meal together is a great way to build such fellowship both in preparation and participation. This helped everyone get involved. Singing together builds unity.

For the study time, we had children, youths, and adults

studying the basic beliefs of the church. Since we had so many from a wide range of traditions, this was a way to share about our beliefs.

Finally, we did something nearly unthinkable. The church still has an aid society that knots comforters for relief. We proposed to have all the children from kindergarten through youth try their hand at it. Soon they learned how to put threaded needles through the comforter and knot the yarn.

The results went far beyond our imagination. In a church with over 140 attending worship services, our family night began to attract more than 100. The meals proved to be a way for many people to become involved in preparation.

I trained table leaders to build a congenial atmosphere around the tables. There was deep sharing in the adult class and a lot of creativity in the children's classes. The youths enjoyed getting together on a regular basis.

The whole intergenerational group also often served by singing for worship services. We had to have the group stand on the side of the sanctuary to fit everyone in. They are called the family night chorale and have offered inspirational songs in worship that arise out of their singing time.

The Mohler family night began with high spirit and has brought movement toward fulfilling the renewal vision.

During times of transition and hardship, servant leaders need to be sensitive to the congregation's present needs without losing track of vision for the future. Perhaps the congregation needs to slow the pace some. Servant leaders can help the group by holding a challenge before them. Challenges can be presented by listening to God and to the needs of the people, and then holding forth vision.

To accomplish vision, we need training. In all aspects of the family night experience, training was part of our plan of implementation. During this time, the leaders in the Mohler renewal movement were trying to be sensitive to the dreams of others, joining with them to plot out the future. As servant leaders, we saw the vision as it could be put into place. We purposed to operate on faith. Leaning into God's grace, we felt that God had more in store for us. God wants us to have wholeness and healing. God has a purpose—that we be a servant people. Often in hardship, we must trim the wick so others can see the light more clearly. Living by faith always brings a risk. In hardship, that risk feels dangerous.

Hardship highlights another central trait of leadership: *foresight.* Robert Greenleaf calls foresight the central ethic of leadership. Foresight is that better-than-average guess about what is going to happen in the future.[63]

The servant has an ear to the ground and lives by vision. There is a gap between what is known and what is sensed, and an envelope of time in which one is yet free to act. Failing to act means that one is merely reacting to situations at hand rather than having the courage to lead into the future. True leaders act on their values and vision, derived from the gospel. Thus foresight entails ethics.

Foresight is an overarching umbrella in the biblical references of Isaiah, Revelation, and John (see chapters 1-3, above, and 8). The prophet Isaiah calls Israel as servant of God to look at the future through the eyes of the past covenant. That is better than making compromises and departing from faith in the Lord and covenant values.

John the Revelator calls the church, surrounded by a wayward society, to faithfulness in following the Lamb and acting from the vision of the new creation. John 13 shows how Jesus, by serving in the present, gives a central model of what the kingdom is to become. In each case, foresight is critical. Ethics is at the heartbeat of living the faith.

In hardship and always, servant leaders learn to keep their vision of the future balanced with needs of the present. Servant leaders consider signals already received. They lead and take initiative at critical moments when they sense the Spirit of God calling them to risk action. Like the Great Pyrenees and Catalan Herder sheepdogs, when they hear the voice of the Shepherd, they respond. They are proactive in accord with values instilled within. They follow ethics because ethics lift up values, values lift up vision, vision lifts up faith, and faith lifts up Jesus Christ. We have to step out in faith and trust in our understanding of God's purposes. Rather than just doing what was always done in the past, we are moving into an uncharted future. Hardship makes one more aware of the uncertainties of life. Hardship can also cause one to become clearer about trusting the leadings of the Spirit. After the renewal movement begins, the church can begin to gain new confidence as assurances of faith become real.

Serving and Manner

Rather than using coercion or force, the servant leader seeks other ways to resolve hardship and conflict. Collaboration and persuasion are two such alternatives. Briefly put, collaboration is a problem-solving process whereby all parties try to work through issues.[64] Persuasion, Webster says, is to "prevail on (a person) to do something, as by advising, urging, etc."[65] Robert Greenleaf on servant leadership and Speed Leas on conflict management point to the use of persuasion.

Leas begins his exposition on persuasion with this statement that sounds much like servant leadership: "Try specifically to meet the needs of the other person or persons who are the target of your persuasive activities."[66] Servants do not necessarily have to be passive but must show respect for other people. Let us look a little further into collaboration first and then persuasion.

Servant leaders will find the collaborative style quite compatible with their traits and goals. It fits well with the listening approach. One attempts to hear the input and feedback of each person. In collaboration, one seeks to join people by finding a way to gather up the concerns and interests of the individual parts. In this mode, the servant leader attempts to help people pull together with each other toward mutual goals.

I found that collaboration often worked well in our youth ministry. I took time to open each meeting with some type of devotional. This set a listening style—listening first to God and to God's movement in our youth work. Then, as issues or agenda items came up, I would attempt to draw forth the ideas of each person. Sometimes this required negotiation. Sometimes it took quite a bit of discussion. I would continually attempt to discern the spirit of the moment and the spirit of our mission.

One time we could not agree on the financial figure to be allotted for cosponsoring the training event at the resource center. One member felt strongly that we should not overextend ourselves in our developing stages. Another member was enthusiastic and willing to take her salary and put it toward the event.

Rather than force the item, I decided that I needed to go back to the sponsoring group and renegotiate the amount of the request. This turned out well: the sponsoring group learned about our development and agreed to a lesser amount. In what turned out to be a lengthy discussion, we learned how individuals perceived our movement as a group. Ultimately, everyone won. In collaboration the sense of "us" grows.

Persuasion can also play a definite role for the servant leader. To persuade someone, leaders need to know that person's interests and needs. Rather than just focusing on their own ideas, servant leaders are sensitive to what the other person wants.

Greenleaf likes to point to John Woolman, who set about to rid the Society of Friends (the Quakers) of slavery. Woolman worked in a gentle manner rather than simply censuring slaveholders. He would ask questions such as what the business of holding slaves does to a person morally and what it means to their children. It took some thirty years to rid the Quakers of slavery, but Woolman finally reached his goal.[67]

By working nonjudgmentally toward the church's goals, the servant leader can help the group move forward and win those who are still questioning what should be done. If vision and needs are being brought together with gentleness and love, people often will be able to get on board with a ministry.

Remember the Servant's gentle manner: "A bruised reed he will not break, and a dimly burning wick he will not quench" (Isa. 42:3). In times of conflict, servant leaders operate gently, from the heart of prayer. This does not mean that they do not get upset, but it does mean that they learn how to channel their anger and to be proactive rather than reactive. In the Servant Songs, the Servant leader operates from the heart of peace. Such leaders share a core of peace with all concerned.

By being aware of different conflict management styles, servant leaders can operate more effectively and make better choices. In all cases, knowing as Isaiah did what it meant to be the underdog, servant leaders do not act negatively. Instead, they lift up those who are hurting. This is their role. They are able to see how others in their weakness can also become servant leaders. They can see the good in others, even "the least and the lost."

In this way, servant leaders can draw forth the talents of each individual by working gently and consistently when hardship arises. They take time to minister to those who are hurting in a situation. Through collaboration and persuasion, they keep working toward their goals.

Unlikely Candidates for Servant Leaders

Hardship often has a way of showing who the servant leaders really are. Sometimes the most unlikely person shines. We noted this in the ropes course ("Creating a Team" in chap. 6). Consider Israel, beaten down and yet called to be a light to the nations (Isa. 49:6). God has a way of using unlikely candidates for the work of the kingdom.

Often through the experience of dealing with prior hardship, real servant leaders can emerge. Hardship has a way of tempering one's spirit, peeling off pretense, molding one into the manner of Christ. True servant leaders show their authenticity when their witness is purified on the anvil of difficulty. Through hardship, one can clarify one's goals. Hardship can be the avenue to maturity.

Whenever hardship occurs, servant leaders listen to all people—even those who they feel do not have the answers. Servant leaders learn that truth often resides, not just in one person, but in the collection of many thoughts. At that point, servant leaders themselves can feel inadequate and may be tempted toward self-rejection.

Henri Nouwen addresses this topic by saying that the greatest trap in life is not success, popularity, or power but self-rejection.[68] Servant leaders can feel their own limitations at such times, but they must also affirm that they are God's beloved. God will give the strength and trust to make it through the difficulty.

When interventions must be made, the servant leader calls on the trust of all. The leader sets up guidelines of what a covenant entails. In accord with Matthew 18:15-20, one goes to another, seeking to build friendship and work out differences. If this does not bring resolution, several people go together, representing the church. Reconciliation is an active process and is primary for building up the body of Christ.

Here again, servant leaders need to be in touch with the movement of God. There is a cost to being a servant leader. Only through self-sacrifice can one be available to serve God. Rather than going it alone, however, the servant discovers that God gives the strength. As with the Servant's call in Isaiah, God goes with the one called. God stays with the one God calls; servant leaders are not left alone. A song on their hearts buoys them up.

In a very practical sense, we have seen throughout this resource that God uses unlikely candidates to learn the heart of the servant. None of the congregations mentioned in this or the earlier resource has anything that would necessarily distinguish them as choice parishes, naturally the places for renewal to occur. None had a huge endowment; none were necessarily in a location that would mean instant growth; none was given a grant to be a pilot project for renewal.

In each case they began to identify a need, felt drawn by God to be useful, took up a leadership style of the servant, formed a team, and began to assess strengths. Like renovating an old house that has endured a lot of hard weather, servant leaders identify the strengths and then the needs and develop a plan. They probably start at a place they sense is the best to begin and for which they have resources to make an impact. They also determine what needs to be done for a next stage to be put into place. Church renewal is much like that—allowing for the serendipity of God breaking in.

As learned in a recent construction project, however, leaders have to begin. Then they might see a whole new avenue emerge along the way. God can use unlikely candidates to be a light. Rather than developing overnight, such a process usually takes at least three years to make an impact and perhaps ten to make any permanent difference. This ten-year concept was learned from senior churchman and peacemaker M. R. Zigler, who came out of retirement to initiate three unthinkable projects. An example of this long-range view is seen in Larry Waltz's renewal project as an executive minister in a region of diverse churches in the Philadelphia area, as highlighted in this book.

Such a long-term approach can be broken down into smaller parts. In church renewal language, we take a year to do all the pre-work, including worksheets 1-7 in the appendix, and to formulate a three-year plan. That plan is then implemented and tracked, encouraged, and evaluated by the envisioning committee. Near the close of three years, an evaluation may be done out of which can arise a new Scripture passage and another three-year plan. Some of that plan may repeat and certainly should build on the first three years. New areas are likely to occur as one explores a new renewal Scripture. Then near the close of that plan, approaching the seventh year, one begins the process afresh. Rather than a quick flash in the pan, renewal is a steady process of growth.

Just as God uses unlikely candidates in terms of the body, so does God lift up some overlooked individuals in the renewal effort, as I have observed happening. This is the whole concept of the one and the many, of the servant being an individual and a body. In the above renewal projects, often some very unlikely individuals come through in ways that might strike one as unusual. I have observed a youth who began to show initiative, a developmentally delayed person who found a niche, an old leader with new fire. Just as in the Bible, God begins to raise up the humble and the unlikely to do the will of the kingdom. Churches and persons who feel inadequate or unworthy are empowered to do God's work as servants.

In a faith orientation, it is natural to return to the springs from where the strength comes. This will be more and more evident as we look at our closing topics.

8
Servant Leadership and Faith Transformation

Our family recently attended a Disaster Relief Sale. Every kind of item imaginable was being auctioned to raise funds for disaster relief around the world. At one point the auctioneer put up an old wooden tub used in church foot-washing services. I was interested but felt I didn't have a chance, yet I put a bid on it—and got it!

As I took the tub back to our seats, I noticed that one rim was missing. I put it down on the floor—and it promptly fell apart into twenty-six pieces! I soon learned that lack of use caused this. The water usually makes the wooden slats swell and keeps it in shape.

Alas! How much this is like the cry of the church for renewal! Renewal comes by restoring the function of the tub. It will take a lot of work to put it all back together—but it is possible.

Many times after a church's decline or devastation the leaders have said, "If only we had listened to the signals." Often the signals that a church is in need and crying out for transformation can be detected early—before the "rim" is completely gone and the "tub" is about to fall apart. Those early signs often emerge as irritation and subtle conflicts or as messages that come back in ways other than how they were sent.

Sagging attendance is often an indicator, of course, and fewer and fewer people doing more and more of the work. One-liners in newsletters or comments that couch frustration are indicators not to be ignored. Perhaps the greatest indicator is loss of vision. Unless vision remains apparent, individuals will lose interest. If these signals are recognized and the problems addressed, new life can emerge.

How can new life emerge? How can a church become transformed? How can people be transformed? So often when we want transformation, we look for some program that promises new life and vitality. We tell ourselves, "Surely if we only find the right program for enough people, things will change." But we have learned that renewal means more than that.

Renewal comes as people are transformed. Marketing strategies go only so far, and the usual managerial and organizational strategies are only partly helpful. At the heart of the church is the ongoing transformation of lives. That points us to biblical values and goals. The power of the gospel is that God re-forms us all and shapes us into servants in God's kingdom. Servant leaders are therefore central to faith transformation and church renewal.

Being Served

Our vision from the outset has been of leadership kneeling by the springs that bring new life. Transformation of individuals and of the church has to do with receiving new life from God, both for servant leaders and for those emerging as fellow servants. Not to be forced or coerced, people receive new life by partaking of the Living Springs.

It is self-limiting for us to think that one can just hold onto or rally the forces for renewal because such movements last only so long. New life can and will happen as people join in receiving the good news of the gospel. Right in the foot washing performed by Jesus, we find the key to transformation.

In John 13 we find the powerful story of Jesus kneeling to wash the feet of his disciples. In this familiar drama, we find some surprising elements that speak of transformation.

During that last week of Jesus' earthly ministry, the city of Jerusalem is teaming with people. Anticipation is running high, for the paschal lamb being sacrificed signifies deliverance. All in the believing community participate and are part of the drama of redemption.

What a time for Jesus to add drama to drama! The paradox of it all is that Jesus sees the drama not in the glory but in the humility of the servant. Rather than an impulse of the moment, Jesus' action arises out of deep love. Jesus kneels before his disciples and washes their feet as a household servant would. Rather than a temporary love, John stresses how Jesus loves them to the end.[69] Jesus knows his journey as a servant, from God and back to God.

This event offers a lesson for servant leaders from Jesus the Mentor. It shows two sides to the faith-transformation experience. When events are in a downward spiral, the pressure can be great to try to make a big splash, to create a miracle. Lofty dreams can be the prelude to greater letdown. At that moment, Jesus remembers from whence he has come and to where he is going. Rather than simply reacting to dark forces plotting his death, he positively loves his followers. Rather than trying to move up in worldly fashion, he kneels. Jesus takes up a towel.

The water of foot washing is a symbol laden with meaning in the Gospel of John. Water is a sign of cleansing, of hope, of new life.[70] Not all are clean, however—and that is the context in which Jesus washes feet. Water won't be enough. More than a quick fix will be needed. Jesus knows that not everyone will come out clean. However, Jesus still washes.

Even for Peter, whom he has to persuade, Jesus washes feet. The persistence of the servant runs throughout this passage. "The washing of the disciples' feet springs from and symbolizes the death and resurrection of Jesus, which both effects the salvation of those whom he loves, and binds them with him in the same humble but victorious destiny."[71]

That evening, people come to supper already bathed. They wear sandals, with feet exposed to the dirt of the street. Only their feet need the attention of the house slave. John, who loves to point to deeper meanings in his Gospel, tells the story of Jesus laying aside his outer robe and taking up the towel. The actions of laying aside and taking up are laden with echoes of death and resurrection.[72]

This is not just some object lesson in humility. This is not the latest cultural transformation theory about some movement of the masses. This is not just an injunction to become more servile, to learn the lessons of being submissive. This passage is not about the "social etiquette" of disciples.[73] "Laying aside" is more costly than choosing to be the last in line at a potluck dinner. It cost Jesus his life.

With the towel of the Roman slave, Jesus starts in his drama. Can you see the amazement? Can you hear any whispers of the disciples? The drama comes to its climax with Peter: "Lord, do you wash my feet?" By placing the pronouns *you* and *my* together, John indicates the forcefulness of Peter's question, contrasting the Master with the disciple. The incongruity of it all is more than Peter can take.

Some interpret this as Peter's pride, yet it also reflects his surprise and perhaps even his wish to keep Jesus from such labor. Besides, if Peter sees Jesus doing this, he knows that to follow Jesus involves the same—doing the work of a servant. Headstrong and intense, Peter finds the act of this drama a bit much to witness, almost too much to receive personally. What will help him understand?

The key is in Jesus' reply. "If I do not wash you, you have no part in me" (John 13:8b). In other words, when we allow Jesus to serve us, we become one with him. This is one side of the transformational experience.

Surely, as John indicates further, they cannot comprehend the full agony of this act in this moment. Who can grasp it in its totality? The full agony of this act cannot be comprehended at once. However, to be washed by Jesus can begin the process, can help bring Peter—and potentially all of us—to be at one with Jesus: one in purpose, one in intent, one in ideals.

Having one's feet washed means to open oneself to the vision of God's kingdom, to be ministered to by Jesus, to receive the cleansing we need every day. Perhaps we can give Peter credit for taking the opportunity on such short notice! For all of his mistakes, that is a sign of real leadership!

Accepting the cleansing or washing is crucial for transformational servant leadership. Religious authenticity grows as people see leaders coming before the Lord to have their feet washed. This does not have to be some verbal and public demonstration of weakness; it can be an action born out of humility that cannot be expressed by words. It may involve an actual foot washing or a similar symbolic action or experience. This is a cleansing of servant leaders to prepare them to serve God and others. Such a washing does not have to be a sad-faced, somber event; it may often have a winsome quality.

Having one's feet washed means to become fit for service. Servants do it for the right motive and to show the bond they have with Jesus. Such service will arise not from its own strength or out of its own insight. Such service comes from the confession that one needs one's own feet washed, and that such an experience commissions one to wash the feet of others.

Transformation originates from the One who transforms. As leaders, we never do the changing. We never have the total power of insight. We never carry the power on our own shoulders. We can merely enter the drama, the first part of which is allowing our feet to be washed.

In this act of surrender, we enter the first part of the paradox of spiritual transformation and servant leadership. In terms of spiritual formation, something fundamental happens when we have our feet washed. To recognize one's own needs at such moments means to hold forth the vision, to embrace the kingdom, and to enter the stream of God's love.

Out of that love and vision, we are enabled both to serve and to lead. Serving originates in our relationship with Christ, in actually receiving his servanthood to and for us. The empowering we have is not in gaining power over others but in receiving the washing and serving from Jesus.

Then we serve the purpose God has given us, and we serve the Savior who washes and renews us. Such a Christ-centeredness has been integral to all servant leadership projects that I have witnessed. Our beliefs come alive as we enter the whole transformation process that is at the heart of renewal of the church. Receiving afresh the cleansing of God can prepare us for service. That moves us to the other side of the transformational experience.

Serving

We must kneel when we wash the feet of others. In that posture, we take on the form of Christ, bending our knees as we wash. In this act, which can be done literally or symbolically, we both serve and effect cleansing for another. Something miraculous happens as we take on that form. We participate in the foot-washing event enacted in symbol and drama. Words cannot gather up all the implications of that simple act. Others change, and we change in so serving.

Churches that live out servant leadership become transformed. The body changes through service, through ministries that are personal in nature, through a project that meets the social needs of our society, or through involvement in missions far or near. In becoming Christ to others, the whole orientation of a congregation changes. We can see this in the way decisions are made, in the character of the people, and in the way relationships are formed. Servants follow in the footsteps of the Master.

The foot-washing service provided a powerful model for the congregation in which I was ordained. An integrated congregation, First Church of the Brethren was the location for a rental union to pool money for housing. Dr. Martin Luther King Jr. had started this union when he went to Chicago. The congregation was vital spiritually, which is why my wife and I went there.

Our minister was black, and the moderator was white. The organist was black, and the choir director was white. In addition to a spiritual rootedness, the church offered vibrant fellowship and opportunities for service ministry. These included the nearby church-related hospital, a drug treatment center, a sewing group for the community, and various other outreach programs.

On the weekend when Martin Luther King Jr. was shot, we held a love feast and communion weekend at our church. Black members encouraged those of us who were white not to attend Sunday morning services due to the fires in Chicago. In fact, a black member who went to get the grape juice for the communion elements was mistaken for a white person and had her car rammed.

However, by Sunday evening, with the National Guard in the streets and the cry of "Whitey, Whitey" in the air, we descended the stairs of old First Church to wash our brothers' and sisters' feet. As I knelt before the black feet in front of me, I thought of what a powerful symbol the foot washing is for our time! Although many churches and other buildings were burned during that time, not one more hole was made in our already-peppered stained-glass windows.

Service becomes the nature and character of the church that decides not to be served but to serve. The service may be in establishing ministries in the church itself or in developing ministries for the community or the world. As the church responds with its strengths to the needs around it, service in the name of Christ is performed.

Something ringing true to faith happens whenever the

church operates in the manner of Christ, who washed the feet of the world. Every action within a renewal plan can be part of kneeling, washing, and drying.

Service requires servants to take initiative, run risks, and sacrifice themselves. Servant leadership is not a weak and passive stance. Service requires servants to follow the kingdom vision and live by Christ's specific call to them. Service is inherent in the nature and character of the church that decides not to be served but to serve.

Servant leadership begins to mold a congregation in its entire being. A certain authenticity and credibility emerges in such a church. Church members start living out their message, and it attracts others. Word and deed become one. The nature of the gospel is experienced. The collective body takes on the form of the servant.

People's lives are changed. They experience the love of Jesus and have their hearts warmed by his love. In serving and being served, two movements of spiritual transformation occur. The transformation at the Living Springs becomes evident in all that permeates the life of such a church.

Empowering Servant Leaders

As we live out servant leadership and develop servant leaders, we all become stronger. The path of servant leadership is continually that of empowering servant leaders. Empowerment extends to actual nurture and training of servant leaders. This means encouraging others as well as calling forth their gifts for the mission at hand.

The whole process of empowering others begins from first welcoming and showing hospitality and proceeds through the actual training and nurture of leaders. So often churches must learn how to be a welcoming place so that the stranger can become a participant and the participant a full partner. Often leadership comes full circle as the newcomer becomes shepherd to ones who welcomed them.

We had an experience with this personally. We arrived at our church camp to go family camping one wet evening. We were trying to figure out how to get settled. How would we ever prepare supper? As we walked around, we were surprised to be greeted by a church I had helped in renewal. They invited us to come over and enjoy some of their stew. Our hearts as well as our stomachs were warmed that evening as we enjoyed stew and fellowship. We dubbed the meal "renewal stew."

Those in renewal extend hospitality. When we held the conference on servant leadership and church renewal, I knew immediately what recipe should be served for lunch. The cooks added their own extra ingredients. Perhaps you can use this recipe for renewal stew when you have a meal with some renewal event:

Brown and add salt and pepper to three pounds of ground beef and two large onions, diced. When cooked, add and simmer: three sixteen-ounce cans of stewed tomatoes, undrained; and two sixteen-ounce cans of light red kidney beans, undrained. Add two sixteen-ounce cans of mixed vegetables, drained. Then add two cups of uncooked Minute Rice. If too thick, add some water. Simmer till all are hot. Add what you want to the stew. As renewal occurs, it just gets better and better!

Servant leaders learn that it is crucial to develop relationships. This comes from welcoming the stranger to fostering relationships within the church and beyond. For example, once I worked with an American Baptist executive minister, Larry Waltz, and four faltering churches. Larry asked whether he could develop his own renewal plan for his diverse district. That seemed like a great idea to me.

He looked for a key Scripture passage to fit the varied population in his churches around Philadelphia. The people needed to learn to relate to each other. So he decided to adopt a passage from Leviticus on extending hospitality (Lev. 19:15-18). He felt that the old biblical imagery of welcoming a stranger into one's tent was just as relevant today as it was in the past. He developed a conference theme on "breaking down the walls" as his emphasis of renewal (cf. Eph. 2:14). What excitement grew out of this vision!

From there, Larry went on to find a new Scripture, Ephesians 2:19-22, to formulate a ten-year theme of renewal for his entire Philadelphia district of American Baptist churches. Larry developed the theme "Household of Faith" to run to the year 2007, reaching their three-hundredth anniversary. Since this was a multicultural, diverse, and independent group, he wanted to enhance the integrity of each of his churches. God keeps the household, he says. So each of the ten years, there is a chosen theme to lift up this overarching vision.

In 1998, they emphasized worship, using traditional hymns, gospel music, and songs of the Taizé community. In 1999, they dipped into the Baptist heritage, using a first-time-ever conference of a host of Baptist groups. For the year 2000, the district is following the theme of the Jubilee, when there is forgiveness and reconciliation of culture and races, highlighting confession, and moving further. This is an excellent example of how an entire district can be guided in renewal out of a scriptural vision.

Relationships are key in renewal. We saw this as we looked at cycles of renewal in working as a team in chapter 6. As Martin Saarinen noted, when on the upswing of the curve of renewal, program often is put ahead of people. This is where decline can set in so rapidly. People and their talents and needs are crucial factors in developing ministries and leadership. There needs to be a balance in considering people needs and program needs. Relationships are primary in this mix.

Much of what we have spoken about in this book entails

developing servant leadership. We will see a definite faith transformation as individuals choose between serving their self-interests and serving the interests of others. However, we need to make a specific effort for servant leadership to develop. Servants realize that to empower leaders, we need to give them the tools they need in their serving.

Calling and developing leaders needs to be monitored for maximum growth to occur. Training becomes important and is part of the process of empowering servant leaders. Those relationships also continue between the training leaders and the servant leaders in training.

Organizationally, one can develop leadership by spreading out responsibility and creating ownership. We continually did this in creating the youth ministry at the Elizabethtown Church. We recognized that the junior high group would need to be adult driven. At first, adults did a lot of the organizing and leading. However, as the year progressed, more and more of the youths took initiative.

As a senior high group developed, we specifically said it should be youth driven. So the cabinet was made up of at least two youths per grade along with four counselors. Young servant leaders emerged as they were motivated to move into serving positions. In the process, they grew spiritually as individuals and as a group.

Developing relationships is key in servant-led structures. As people are encouraged in their strengths, bonds develop. Servant leaders foster relationships and offer love and support. As people deal with their weaknesses, they become motivated to offer their talents. Servant structures have an interdependency among members. Sometimes in serving and sometimes in being served, members use their mutually beneficial talents. Something spiritual happens as those kind of relationships develop. Servant leaders see the value in the spirit of cooperation.

Servant leaders help us see that indeed more is needed if we are led by our vision. Servant leaders see that they are indeed modeling the very thing they hope others will take up. The test of that serving is that others will become servants. Thus we anticipate that they will become the kind of leaders who will be a real blessing in the church. Nurturing leaders readies one for renewal. Because servants are trying to help other people, the church receives many blessings and dividends from this investment.

Empowering others involves appointing them to function as elders. An exemplary act of choosing elders occurred when Jethro gave instructions to his son-in-law Moses (Exod. 18). The people recognized that the elders held a position of leadership and authority. They shared wisdom to help God's people. Elders were representing and maintaining the community.[74]

Various students in church renewal courses pick up the instructions Jethro gave Moses when he was feeling so weighed down. Some entire renewal projects have come out of this vision. Because of the impact that this Scripture has had in church renewal projects and the sharing and building of leadership, this elder's vision bears quoting:

"What is this that you are doing for the people? Why do you sit alone, and all the people stand about you from morning till evening?"

And Moses said to his father-in-law, "Because the people come to me to inquire of God; when they have a dispute, they come to me and I decide between a man and his neighbor, and I make them know the statutes of God and his decisions."

Moses' father-in-law said to him, "What you are doing is not good. You and the people with you will wear yourselves out, for the thing is too heavy for you; you are not able to perform it alone. Listen now to my voice; I will give you counsel and God be with you!

"You shall represent the people before God, and bring their cases to God; and you shall teach them the statutes and the decisions, and make them know the way in which they must walk and what they must do. "Moreover choose able men from all the people, such as fear God, men who are trustworthy and who hate a bribe; and place such men over the people as rulers of thousands, of hundreds, of fifties and of tens. And let them judge the people at all times; every great matter they shall bring to you, but any small matter they shall decide themselves; so it will be easier for you, and they will bear the burden with you. "If you do this, and God so commands you, then you will be able to endure, and all this people also will go to their place in peace." (Exod. 18:14-23)

This is not just good management in ancient formation. The whole role of eldering also has a great spiritual thread running throughout it as well. A Presbyterian student in a church renewal course entered from an interesting track of ministry. As a professional interim pastor, she goes from one interim position to another. Rather than just filling the pulpit and making no changes, she leads congregations into a deeper spiritual walk.

As part of her doctor of ministry program, she explored the role of elders biblically and historically. She found that elders had a largely spiritual task. The term *elder* translates the Greek term *presbyteros* (1 Tim. 5:17-22; 1 Pet. 5:1-5; Acts 14:23; 20:17; et al.). This leadership function is to nurture others spiritually and not just to govern the church.

She identified this insight as crucial if the church is to survive. She felt deeply that the church needs to help people with the deeper issues of biblical spirituality. Thus all members, including designated leaders, feel that they are growing spiritually and have a spiritual role to fulfill.

One day this student asked to be excused from attending one of the upcoming classes. She had led a spiritual retreat for some members of the church, and the board had heard of it. They too wanted a spiritual retreat, and the only suitable time she could not find conflicted with class.

How could I deny such a request, especially in a course on church renewal! What potential there is for all of the church to be renewed and to grow in leadership. It all begins with thirsting for the Living Waters and sharing those Living Waters with others.

In this process of renewal, we should continually see how to nurture, train, and enlist leaders. If a congregational meeting to identify strengths is being held or some other project is launched, it is good to pair a veteran leader with an individual who may serve as a leader in training. They could be called coleaders because seasoned leaders always know they can learn, especially as they train others.

The relationships help a team expand and grow. Thus the bond is built that can sustain a ministry when the ups and downs come along. For that, let us turn once more to the Living Springs and see how that water can bring new life.

Refreshing at the Springs

"The water that I will give will become in them a spring of water gushing up to eternal life," says Jesus (John 4:14, NRSV). What beautiful words of inspiration and encouragement! In speaking them to the woman at the well, Jesus ensures her of fulfillment for the deep needs in her heart for all eternity. As she speaks with Jesus, she likely is not even totally aware of what her needs are. Through him, however, she discovers fulfillment that can offer so much to herself and her neighbors.

Water has been the thematic word running throughout this resource. Servanthood has been the modality. Whether in the lesson from Isaiah, the book of Revelation, or the Gospel of John, we have observed and come to understand how the servant leader's manner and style developed. We have also explored how servanthood intersects with spirituality. Through being served, and as we ourselves kneel to serve others, we have discovered the mystery of the Christian life and the way of renewal in the church.

Let's look a little more deeply into this spiritual connection by exploring the way in which waters convey the symbol of life.

In the Old Testament, springs are not just sources of water but locations of theophanies, revelations of God.[75] In a beautiful story in the Bible, Abraham's servant is sent out to find a wife for Isaac. The servant promises to find someone from Abraham's kindred, one from whom his descendants would come.

At the well near Nahor, the servant knows he has found her when at his request she gives him a drink of water and then offers to water his camels. The girl, Rebekah, is given a choice of whether or not to go with Abraham's servant. She agrees to go because she believes that this is all God's doing (Gen. 24). Israel's fountain is the Lord, and refreshment comes from that fountain (cf. Jer. 2:13; 17:13).

In the New Testament, Jesus distinguishes between the water he can give and the water of Jacob's well (John 4). The water from Jesus quenches spiritual thirst. Possession of this water means abiding fellowship with Christ. The water from Jesus will gush up to eternal life, something the believer already participates in, according to the Gospel of John.

In Revelation the reference to springs of the water of life has an eschatological connotation (7:17; 21:6; cf. 22:1, 17). It also refers to the consummation that Christ will bring at the last day.[76]

Servants have an awesome task, then, to be channels of the living water. Today's servant leaders are still refreshed at that well from God. While they may feel inadequate for their mission, they are given strength as they drink from the springs. Servant leaders are not weak leaders; they feel guided by their call.

As they learn to be sustained at the Living Springs, they

also learn how to catch a vision, build a team, and put ministries into practice. The process may be costly; risk is involved and courage is needed. But servant leaders feel a power they cannot explain. They are refreshed as they turn to the One who calls them in mission.

Servants who are shepherds by the Living Springs help congregations become more serving. This means taking up ministries that serve within and beyond their walls. Ministries happen inside congregational life itself and when members are serving in various arenas of life.

Just as the Servant in the Servant Songs is both the one and the many, in the church today both individuals and the corporate whole take on the character of service. Such service has a character of sensitivity to others, coloring all the church's ministries. In other words, the body begins to take on a servant motif, and its ministries begin to take on a life-giving quality.

In our development of youth ministries at Elizabethtown, we organized a younger group for grades three to five. At first the leaders thought they would plan just social activities, since the children had Sunday school classes. This would help them build relationships. However, it was soon discovered that to have balance, they needed some service projects.

The children served by visiting the nearby nursing home and providing encouragement to residents. The group took on a whole new character as they developed a more well-rounded program.

Shepherds by the Living Springs uphold values and ethics. When values drive structure, when values drive life, then productivity is felt. For servant leaders who follow the way of Christ, drinking at the Living Springs is crucial. New life then gushes forth at every opportunity. They are bound to take up leadership in other capacities. All that is done and said is tied into the new life springing forth. A broad range of ministries often results—and renewed excitement and commitment as well!

Service means more than just helping others who are destitute. It entails anything that servants do to share their talents. It means reaching out to new people, being a greeter, or helping in the community, or in one's vocation, home, or school. It means reaching out in one's daily rounds. It involves anything that servants do to share their talents.

Such service is more the tone of the sharing than the exact thing that is done. Service takes one into many arenas of life. Tapping into the Living Springs results in people feeling renewed as they are sharing with others their new life in Christ, the ultimate Servant Leader.

Servant leaders, in all they say and do, go on the way with a clear call. As shepherds by the Living Springs, they help the church to become a serving people in word and deed, within their walls and beyond. Servant leadership helps the church to be renewed in what it is called to be.

May the shepherds by the Living Springs be renewed and help to renew others to newness of life in Christ! Amen.

Worksheet 1

A Deeper Spiritual Walk

1. What inner promptings of the Spirit do you feel are calling forth new life in you? How does that lead you toward renewal, personally and congregationally?

2. What sense of calling do you feel for renewal? How can you respond to those promptings and set a course in that direction?

3. Who else might join you in this deeper walk of faith? How might you include them in a special emphasis?

4. What spiritual disciplines would aid you in your journey? Identify resources, format, and time allotment. Could a biblical exploration, quiet time, and writing of a journal of renewal be included?

5. Where do you sense God speaking? What grace is being revealed? What calling for renewal is being felt by you and others?

6. Where do you feel the journey of a deeper spiritual walk is leading you and your congregation? What are you hearing in your time of prayer? Where do you feel God's leadings are taking you now?

7. What biblical text or texts have become especially moving to you in this process? What do you sense renewal means? How is renewal an ongoing process for you now?

Worksheet 2

Moving Toward a Biblical Vision

1. Identify what has drawn you to this text. In this text, what sense of call to renewal or beliefs or values of faith resonate with you?

2. Explore more deeply the meanings of this text. Check each question with various readings of the text and with the use of biblical helps.

• What is the setting in life of the text and how does that life situation speak to your life situation?

• What key words jump out at you? Look up the meanings of those words. How do the meanings of those words speak to you?

• What themes are in the text? How do these themes speak to you? In the midst of your life, where do these words speak of promise and hope?

• What is the gospel here, the good news? From what bondage do these words release you and your congregation? To what new life do they invite you?

3. What dynamics of renewal arise for you from this text? What dynamics of renewal are present for your congregation?

• What dichotomies exist in this text? What paradoxes?

• What sequences? What aspects of renewal are lifted up?

4. Sum up a theme or vision from this text.

• Is there a key word or a theme that leaps forth from this text for renewal?

5. How can you go from here to explore this biblical text

as some expression of a vision for renewal?

6. How may these dynamics of renewal begin to enrich and guide your approach?

• Do you see any initial way in which such a vision may become practical reality? What would be the first small step in implementation?

7. How can you share this vision with your congregation or district? How could you enlist them as a team to explore this text more deeply and with you develop an emerging vision?

Worksheet 3

Developing a Team

1. To begin, enlist God on your team. In prayer with people called together, search out the movement of God and the sense of God knitting and joining you as a team. Take time to receive help from God's Spirit and a sense of God's guidance.

2. Acknowledge that before you is a challenge bigger than yourselves. What needs to be done cannot be done alone. Affirm that the whole (the team) is greater than the sum of its parts (the individuals). This is kingdom arithmetic, with God's wonderful work producing a geometric yield (cf. Mark 4:8).

3. Anticipate that God will move you toward a vision. This is not simply one leader's vision or a group vision but God's vision. Using a biblical passage, try to discern God's call. See that more is possible. Claim Christ's call.

4. Clarify your values. Regarding the purpose of this team, what is important to you? Identify how this team will embody those values. If in conflict, do you have a shared vision or are there conflicting values at work? What united call can be affirmed?

5. Talk over what it means to be a team. On a team there is an all-hands-on-deck policy. If a job needs to be done, each team member says, "I am here, and I will do it unless that job is designated for another or needs to be delegated." In other words, everyone is responsible to get the job done.

6. Teams work best which build on the strengths of each individual. Can you identify the various strengths and gifts of each person and how the team can yoke strengths together and use gifts? How can you compensate for gaps or

weaknesses? Who is versatile on the team and can shift from one task to another?

7. Examine how you are going to work together. How will you plan your work? Will there be meetings? Where is the work done? Is there preparation for a meeting?

8. Is there follow-up work? How does that work get done? Where do you get resources to do the projects? What timetables are projected? Who is expected to take initiative, for what task, and with what support?

9. How will you function when one gets tired or cannot do a job? How will you handle getting impatient with one another? How will your team encourage one another? How will you forgive one another?

10. Teams can and should model the vision that they hope to accomplish. How can this team intentionally model vision? Is there a special spirit to this effort?

11. How are decisions made? Is there discussion? Is there a vote, or are decisions made by consensus? Do you wait upon God's leading and then use a process of spiritual discernment? How does one disagree? How is diversity a gift?

12. How will the team celebrate? How will the team share the pain and share the gain? Is there a way that renewal is built-in from the start? When and where will the rest times come? Where are the springs that renew?

Worksheet 4

Assessment of Strengths

This worksheet is for a group discernment process including as many people in the congregation as possible. A time of devotions may begin this process, setting the posture for listening to God's grace extending to us. The first three questions can be used in small groups and the remainder in a total group experience. The final one may be used by a follow-up team that builds upon this experience.

1. What experiences in this church have been life-changing for you? These may be small or large things, but ones that have made an impression and have been formative for you. What made such an impact?

2. In what experiences was your faith life touched? What about those experiences is meaningful for you? What makes such experiences possible?

3. What strengths can you affirm in your church? How do these strengths play themselves out in experiences?

4. As you look at these strengths as a total group, list common denominators that have bolstered the faith of people and made for growth (on newsprint or blackboard).

5 Out of these factors, identify common themes that point to the unique identity of this congregation. Look for the gifts that God has given to be shared.

6. Make a list of those strengths (on newsprint.) You may conclude with a worship session, with people thanking God for the strengths of this congregation.

7. How can we build on these strengths and factors for growth to meet the identified needs, as God calls us?

Worksheet 5

Assessment of Needs

As a total group or in the renewal team, people can assess current needs to which the strengths can be linked. In such an exercise, the leader may again place the items on newsprint so they are clearly visible.

1. When you think of this congregation, what evident needs come to mind?

2. Where do people hurt? What do people long for?

3. As you are among the people of the congregation and in the community, what are the open and receptive areas where ministry is needed?

4. What needs can you meet by being faithful to your biblical calling and using your strengths?

5. Use the triangle below to envision a plan of renewal. Place your biblical calling on one angle, strengths on another, and evident church and community needs on the third. Look into the center and see where there can be responsiveness in ministry and movement of renewal (see worksheet 7 for further instructions).

Biblical Calling

Spiritual
Growth &
Church Renewal

Strengths   Evident Needs

Servant Leadership

Out of an intense study of the Servant Songs in Isaiah and passages in the New Testament, we find the following seven traits of servant leadership:

1. Servant leaders feel a sense of calling to serve God. God has a purpose for them: to mediate covenant and bring others into God's will. They do this through becoming servants. This is what defines them. Servant leaders serve from a spiritual understanding.

2. Servant leaders are recognized by their manner. Rather than overpowering those already weakened, they work in a humble manner. "A bruised reed he will not break, and a dimly burning wick he will not quench" (Isa. 42:3).

3. Servant leaders lead from a heart of peace. So much of leadership is connecting people with what is happening within, discerning gifts, and connecting them in ministry. This trait can be costly, entailing self-sacrifice. True servants are suffering servants, as in Isaiah 53, because self-emptying before God is part of their essence.

4. Servant leaders have clear vision and lead people to find a vision together. Repeatedly the Servant Songs of Second Isaiah echo a tremendous vision of one called by God for a purpose: to establish justice or a right-ordered society. This mission extends to being a light to all nations (Isa. 49:6).

5. Servants listen. In the third song (Isaiah 50:4-11), the Lord actually opens the Servant's ear every morning. Servanthood originates with attentiveness to God in prayer and word and draws everyone to that attentiveness.

Listening to God helps people develop a sense of how God is helping them meet the needs of those around them.

6. Servant leaders do not characteristically have a spectacular appearance. They don't dress for success. Usually one associates beauty with success, but God uses the unlikely and unlovely to accomplish his work.

7. The last trait builds on all the others. In apparent weakness, the power of God is revealed. Even those delivered are astonished that the Servant is the one who inaugurated their release. The Servant through suffering obtains life. In that, there is an element of surprise and victory. In that sense, there is a song in their hearts. Servants feel a lift, a sense of God at work, and there is joy as expressed in Isaiah 55:12 (NRSV):

> You shall go out in joy,
>   and be led back in peace;
> the mountains and the hills before you
>   shall burst into song,
> and all the trees of the field shall clap their hands.

Worksheet 7

Envisioning a Plan of Renewal

1. You have assessed strengths and factors that make up your congregation's identity. Which needs can be served out of your sense of vision and mission? List those needs.

2. How can vision and strengths and needs be brought together to follow a good direction? Place these three at the points of a triangle, with vision at the apex, strengths on another angle, and needs on the other base angle. Then look into the center for a way into a plan for renewal.

3. How do you "see things whole," looking about three to four years down the road? What dynamics of renewal from your biblical text indicate what that would involve? Where do you sense God is leading? Listen deeply.

4. Beginning with the present, what is the first tiny step toward vision, then the next step that builds upon that one, and so on? In looking at this progression, what would have to wait for attention till something else happened first?

5. What priorities need to be set? What items put on hold? Is there room for the spontaneous to emerge?

6. Put all this on a horizontal time line of fall and spring semesters each year. Put blocks of renewal in place, one after the other. What other steps need to be added?

7. On the time line, outline the overall vision at the far right. Then (left to right) show intermediate steps leading to that point. How can a natural progression of planning be established? What needs to be started in one semester so an emphasis can be launched in the next? Where will there be times for rest, evaluation, and celebration?

Worksheet 8

Implementing a Plan of Renewal

1. Envision each smaller step or block in the overall design. Name smaller components and show how they fit together. What needs to be done for this to develop?

2. What resources must be pulled together to make this work, such as people, books, materials, or experiences?

3. Who needs to be enlisted to accomplish this? How and when can key people sit down and share the vision and what gifts are needed? How can these gifts be offered to accomplish this mission? Who else is needed?

4. How will the little ones in the congregation be regarded in this plan? Who may feel left out of this vision? How can they be accommodated and their strengths used?

5. What training needs to be done? Provide lead time for preparation. What tools will be on hand for carrying out this ministry? What extra resources are needed just in case?

6. What promotion is needed? How can that be done in multiple ways in several media, and repeatedly followed up to reinforce the program plans?

7. From the chart, sketch a smaller module. Put the specific program vision on the right and left-to-right steps leading to that point. What is a natural progression to reach this goal? Allow times for rest, evaluation, and celebration.

8. Spiritual formation happens as vision turns into reality. How will spiritual and practical help be used in regular supervision of this project? Can mentors be enlisted to work with each leader? How will your church thank God for leadings and strength, and give prayer support for leaders and helpers?

Notes

Preface
1. David S. Young, "Marks of Ministry," *Messenger*, 1987.
2. For more information, contact The Robert K. Greenleaf Center for Servant-Leadership, 921 East 86th St., Ste. 200, Indianapolis, IN 46240.

Introduction
3. Louie W. Attebery, *Sheep May Safely Graze* (Moscow, Idaho: Univ. of Idaho Press, 1992), 9.
4. M. E. Ensminger, *The Complete Book of Dogs* (New York: A. S. Barnes & Co., 1977), 76-77; Gino Pugnetti, *Simon and Schuster's Guide to Dogs*, ed. Mondadori (New York: Simon & Schuster, 1980), Dog 10; Bonnie Wilcox and Chris Walkowicz, *Atlas of Dog Breeds* (Neptune City, N.J.: TFH Pubns., 1989).
5. See James Bryan Smith, *A Spiritual Formation Workbook* (San Francisco: Harper, 1991), who builds on Richard Foster, *Celebration of Discipline* (New York: Harper & Row, 1978).

1. A Vision for Leadership
6. Bernhard Anderson, *Understanding the Old Testament*, 2d ed. (Englewood Cliffs: Prentice Hall, 1957), 187-188.
7. See Dietrich Bonhoeffer, *Life Together* (New York: Harper & Row, 1954).
8. Robert K. Greenleaf, *The Servant as Leader* (Cambridge: Center for Applied Studies, 1970), 7.
9. Anderson, 395.
10. Rita J. Burns, *Exodus, Leviticus, Numbers, with Excursus on Feasts, Ritual, Typology*, Old Testament Message Series, 3 (Wilmington: Michael Glazier, 1983), 189-191.
11. Anderson, 394.
12. Claus Westermann, *Isaiah 40-66: A Commentary*, trans. D. M. Stalker, Old Testament Library (Philadelphia: Westminster, 1995), 229.
13. Greenleaf, 10.

2. Leading for Spiritual Growth

14. See David S. Young *A New Heart and a New Spirit: A Plan for Renewing Your Church* (Valley Forge, Pa.: Judson, 1994), 5.

15. For a complementary explanation of these steps in a general church renewal description, see Young, *A New Heart.*

3. Shepherds by the Living Springs

16. May sermon by David S. Young, Drexel Hill Church of the Brethren, in the Easter season.

17. Rev. 1:9; see Vernard Eller, *The Most Revealing Book of the Bible: Making Sense Out of Revelation* (Grand Rapids: Eerdmans, 1974), 41-51.

18. Eller, 71.

19. David J. Wieand, *Visions of Glory* (Elgin: The Brethren Press, 1979), 39-40.

20. Wieand, 40.

21. Second Isaiah was written in the company of priestly writers, who reached back to creation to speak about life. For them, life was always closely related to worship. The book of Revelation has these same features.

22. Young, *A New Heart,* xii, 72-76.

23. See the earlier similar vision for worship in Isaiah 6, and the traditional fivefold pattern suggested for prayer and worship.

24. Reginald Heber, in *The Brethren Hymnal* (Elgin: Brethren Publishing House, 1951), no. 1.

25. Eller, 57.

26. See the excellent resources on discipling by David Lowes Watson, *Covenant Discipleship: Christian Formation Through Mutual Accountability* (Nashville: Discipleship Resources, 1989).

27. George Adam Smith, quoted in William Barclay, *The Revelation of John,* vol. 2, 2d ed. (Philadelphia: Westminster, 1960), 47.

28. Willard Roth, "Mother Teresa," *Courier* 10/2:2.

29. David S. Young, "Sunday Schools That Transform," *Builder,* Feb. 1989, 11-19.

30. See Marlene Kropf and Eddy Hall, *Praying with the Anabaptists: The Secret of Bearing Fruit* (Newton: Faith & Life Press, 1994).

31. See David S. Young, "How the Pastor Can Help Motivate and Supervise Renewal in the Local Congregation," unpublished D.Min. thesis, Bethany Theological Seminary, May 1976, 39.

32. John M. Drescher, *If I Were Starting My Ministry Again: Timeless Instructions and Life-Changing Wisdom* (Nashville: Abingdon, 1995), 68-72.

33. See Wilhelm Michaelis, in *Theological Dictionary of the New Testament*, vol. 6, ed. G. Kittel and G. Friedrich, trans. G. W. Bromiley (Grand Rapids: Eerdmans, 1968), 117.

34. See William F. Arndt and F. Wilbur Gingrich, *A Greek-English Lexicon of the New Testament and Other Early Christian Literature* (Chicago: Univ. of Chicago Press, 1957), 337.

4. Servant Leadership and Approaching Renewal

35. Stephen F. Dintaman, "A Meditation on the Church: Ice, Water, and Pickup Trucks," *Gospel Herald*, June 20, 1995, 1-3.

36. David S. Young, *James: Faith in Action*, Covenant Bible Studies (Elgin: Brethren Press, 1992), 60ff.

37. Young, *A New Heart*, 8-10.

38. For an approach to this gap, which can be seen as a discrepancy, see Lyle Schaller, *Strategies for Change* (Nashville: Abingdon, 1993), 53ff.

39. Young, "How . . . Renewal in the Local Congregation," 46-51.

40. Greenleaf, *The Servant as Leader*, 35.

41. Greenleaf, 1-2.

42. See Walt Mueller, *Understanding Today's Youth Culture* (Wheaton, Ill.: Tyndale House, 1994), and contact his Center for Youth and Parent Understanding, Elizabethtown, Pa.

5. Servant Leadership and Organizing for Renewal

43. Young, *A New Heart*, 79-83.

44. For what Robert Greenleaf calls conceptualizing as the prime leadership talent, see *The Servant as Leader*, 23ff.

45. For a good overview of worship, see Robert E. Webber, *Worship, Old and New* (Grand Rapids: Zondervan, 1994); and James F. White, *Introduction to Christian Worship* (Nashville: Abingdon, 1980).

46. See James Forbes, *The Holy Spirit and Preaching* (Nashville: Abingdon, 1989).

47. Annual Conference, pastors' meetings, Charlotte, North Carolina, 1995.

48. See Richard S. Armstrong, *Service Evangelism* (Philadelphia: Westminster, 1979).

49. See Steve Sjogren, *Conspiracy of Kindness: A Refreshing New Approach to Sharing the Love of Jesus with Others* (Ann Arbor: Servant Publications, 1993).

50. Greenleaf, 23-25.

51. Contact Logos System Associates, 1405 Frey Rd., Pittsburgh, PA 15235.

52. An entire process for such supervisory meetings is given in Young, *A New Heart*, 45-55.

6. Servant Leadership and Servant Structures

53. Susan Bame Hoover, *Faith the Cow* (Elgin: Brethren Press, 1995).

54. For more information on how you can be part of HPI and its worldwide work, you may contact Heifer Project International, P.O. Box 808, Little Rock, AR 72203.

55. Adopted by the HPI Board of Directors, Oct. 3, 1992.

56. See "Plan for Ministry Formulated from Church Goals," in Young, "How . . . Renewal in the Local Congregation," 43-44.

57. See George Parson and Speed Leas, *Understanding Your Congregation as a System* (Washington, D.C.: The Alban Institute, 1993).

58. Martin Saarinen, *The Life Cycle of a Congregation* (Washington, D.C.: The Alban Institute, 1986), 10.

59. See the *Journal of Stewardship*, ed. Sue Whiteset and Phil Williams, published annually for ministers and other church leaders, by the Ecumenical Center for Stewardship Studies, 1100 West 42nd St., Ste. 225, Indianapolis, IN 46208.

60. Richard E. Rusbuldt, *A Workbook on Biblical Stewardship* (Grand Rapids: Eerdmans, 1994), 24-25.

7. Servant Leadership and Handling Hardship

61. Thomas J. Peters and Robert H. Waterman Jr., *In Search of Excellence: Lessons from America's Best-Run Companies* (New York: Harper & Row, 1982).

62. Logos Systems Associates, 1405 Frey Rd., Pittsburgh, PA 15235.

63. Greenleaf, *The Servant as Leader*, 16.

64. Speed Leas, *Discover Your Conflict Management Style* (Washington, D.C.: The Alban Institute, 1984), 17-18.

65. *Webster's New Universal Unabridged Dictionary* (New York: Barnes & Noble, 1989), 1076.

66. Speed Leas, 9.

67. Greenleaf, 29-30.

68. Henri J. M. Nouwen, *Life of the Beloved: Spiritual Living in a Secular World* (New York: Crossroad Publishing Co., 1993), 27.

8. Servant Leadership and Faith Transformation

69. John Marsh, *The Gospel of Saint John,* The Pelican Commentary (Baltimore: Penguin Books, 1968), 484.

70. John Marsh, *Saint John,* 485.

71. John Marsh, 487.

72. John Marsh, 484.

73. John Marsh, 486.

74. See G. Henton Davies, "Elder in the Old Testament," in *The Interpreter's Dictionary of the Bible,* ed. G. A. Buttrick (New York: Abingdon, 1962), 2:72-73.

75. W. L. Reed, "Fountain," in *The Interpreter's Dictionary of the Bible,* 2:323.

76. Wilhelm Michaelis, "Pēgē in the New Testament," *Theological Dictionary of the New Testament,* 6:115-117.

Bibliography

Anderson, Bernhard. *Understanding the Old Testament.* 2d ed. Englewood Cliffs: Prentice Hall, 1957.

Armstrong, Richard S. *Service Evangelism.* Philadelphia: Westminster, 1979.

Arndt, William F., and F. Wilbur Gingrich. *A Greek-English Lexicon of the New Testament and Other Early Christian Literature.* Chicago: Univ. of Chicago Press, 1957.

Attebery, Louie W. *Sheep May Safely Graze: A Personal Essay on Tradition and a Contemporary Sheep Ranch.* A Publication in Northwest Folklife. Moscow, Idaho: Univ. of Idaho Press, 1992.

Bailey, Keith M. *Servants in Charge.* Camp Hill, Pa.: Christian Pubns., 1979.

Barclay, William. *The Revelation of John.* 2 vols. 2d ed. The Daily Study Bible. Philadelphia: Westminster, 1960.

Bauman, Harold E. *Congregations and Their Servant Leaders: Some Aids for Faithful Congregational Relationships.* Scottdale, Pa.: Mennonite Publishing House, 1982.

Bonhoeffer, Dietrich. *Life Together.* New York: Harper & Row, 1954.

Burns, Rita J. *Exodus, Leviticus, Numbers, with Excursus on Feasts, Ritual, Typology.* Old Testament Message Series, 3. Wilmington: Michael Glazier, 1983.

Buttrick, G. A., ed. *The Interpreter's Dictionary of the Bible.* 4 vols. New York: Abingdon, 1962. *Suppl.*, ed. K. Crim, Nashville: Abingdon, 1976.

Dintaman, Stephen F. "A Meditation on the Church: Ice, Water, and Pickup Trucks." *Gospel Herald*, June 20, 1995, 1-3.

Dobbins, Richard. "Creative Management of Conflict," a tape recording. Akron, Ohio: Emerge Ministries.

Drescher, John M. *If I Were Starting My Ministry Again: Timeless Instructions and Life-Changing Wisdom.* Nashville: Abingdon, 1995.

Eller, Vernard. *The Most Revealing Book of the Bible: Making Sense Out of Revelation.* Grand Rapids: Eerdmans, 1974.

Forbes, James. *The Holy Spirit and Preaching.* Nashville: Abingdon, 1989.

Foster, Richard J. *Celebration of Discipline: The Path to Spiritual Growth.* New York: Harper & Row, 1978; rev. ed., HarperSanFrancisco, 1988.

Greenleaf, Robert K. *The Servant as Leader.* Cambridge: Center for Applied Studies, 1970.

_____. *Servant Leadership: A Journey into the Nature of Legitimate Power and Greatness.* Mahwah, N.J.: Paulist Press, 1977.

Hoover, Susan Bame. *Faith the Cow.* Elgin: Brethren Press, 1995.

Interpreter's Dictionary of the Bible. See Buttrick.

Journal of Stewardship. See Whiteset.

Kittel, G., and G. Friedrich, eds. *Theological Dictionary of the New Testament.* Trans. and ed. G. W. Bromiley, vols. 1-9. Index, vol. 10, compl. R. Pitkin. Grand Rapids: Eerdmans, 1964-76.

Kropf, Marlene, and Eddy Hall. *Praying with the Anabaptists: The Secret of Bearing Fruit.* Newton: Faith & Life Press, 1994.

Leas, Speed. *Discover Your Conflict Management Style.* Washington, D.C.: The Alban Institute, 1984.

Marsh, John. *The Gospel of Saint John.* The Pelican Commentary. Baltimore: Penguin Books, 1968.

Mead, Loren. *The Once and Future Church: Reinventing the Congregation for a New Mission Frontier.* Washington, D.C.: The Alban Institute, 1991.

Mueller, Walt. *Understanding Today's Youth Culture.* Wheaton, Ill.: Tyndale House, 1994.

Mulholland, M. Robert. *Revelation: Holy Living in an Unholy World.* Grand Rapids: Zondervan, 1990.

Nouwen, Henri J. M. *Life of the Beloved: Spiritual Living in a Secular World.* New York: Crossroad Publishing Co., 1993.

O'Connor, Elizabeth. *Servant Leaders, Servant Structures.* Washington, D.C.: Servant Leadership, 1991.

Parson, George, and Speed Leas. *Understanding Your Congregation as a System.* Washington, D.C.: The Alban Institute, 1993.

Peters, Thomas J., and Robert H. Waterman Jr. *In Search of Excellence: Lessons from America's Best-Run Companies.* New York: Harper & Row, 1982.

Roth, Willard. *"Mother Teresa." Courier* 10/2.

Rusbuldt, Richard E. *A Workbook on Biblical Stewardship.* Grand Rapids: Eerdmans, 1994.

Saarinen, Martin. *The Life Cycle of a Congregation.* Washington, D.C.: The Alban Institute, 1986.

Schaller, Lyle E. *Strategies for Change.* Nashville: Abingdon, 1993.

Sjogren, Steve. *Conspiracy of Kindness: A Refreshing New Approach to*

Sharing the Love of Jesus with Others. Ann Arbor: Servant Publications, 1993.

Smith, James Bryan. *A Spiritual Formation Workbook.* San Francisco: Harper, 1991.

Theological Dictionary of the New Testament. See Kittel.

Watson, David Lowes. *Covenant Discipleship: Christian Formation Through Mutual Accountability.* Nashville: Discipleship Resources, 1989.

Webber, Robert E. *Worship, Old and New.* Grand Rapids: Zondervan, 1994.

Westermann, Claus. *Isaiah 40-66: A Commentary.* Trans. D. M. Stalker. Old Testament Library. Philadelphia: Westminster, 1995.

White, James F. *Introduction to Christian Worship.* Nashville: Abingdon, 1980.

Whiteset, Sue, and Phil Williams, eds. *Journal of Stewardship.* Indianapolis: Ecumenical Center for Stewardship Studies, annual.

Wieand, David J. *Visions of Glory.* Elgin: The Brethren Press, 1979.

Young, David S. "How the Pastor Can Help Motivate and Supervise Renewal in the Local Congregation." D.Min. thesis, Bethany Theological Seminary, May 1976.

_____ *James: Faith in Action.* Covenant Bible Studies. Elgin: Brethren Press, 1992.

_____ "Marks of Ministry." *Messenger,* 1987.

_____ *A New Heart and a New Spirit: A Plan for Renewing Your Church.* Valley Forge: Judson, 1994.

_____ "Sunday Schools That Transform." *Builder,* Feb. 1989, 11-19.

Further Resources

Consulting and Resourcing

The Alban Institute, 7315 Wisconsin Ave., Suite 1250 W, Bethesda, MD 20814-3211 (800-486-1318).

New Life Ministries, 1996 Donegal Springs Rd., Mt. Joy, PA 17552 (800-774-3360; lifeminncw@aol.com).

Many districts, judicatories, national offices, and seminaries are developing resource centers. Network to find them.

Readings on Servant Leadership

Bauman, Harold E. *Congregations and Their Servant Leaders: Some Aids for Faithful Congregational Relationships.* Scottdale, Pa.: Mennonite Publishing House, 1982.

Greenleaf, Robert K. *The Power of Servant Leadership.* San Francisco: Berrett-Koehler, 1998.

_____. *Seeker and Servant.* San Francisco: Jossey Bass, 1996.

_____. *Servant Leadership: A Journey into the Nature of Legitimate Power and Greatness.* Mahwah, N.J.: Paulist Press, 1977.

O'Connor, Elizabeth. *Servant Leaders, Servant Structures.* Washington, D.C.: Servant Leadership, 1991.

Spears, Larry, ed. *Insights on Leadership.* New York: John Wiley, 1998.

Training in Church Renewal

Doctor of Ministry program for renewing churches, Eastern Baptist Theological Seminary, 6 Lancaster Ave., Wynnewood, PA 19096 (800-220-3287; www.ebts.edu).

Doctor of Ministry programs can be tailored for unique features like urban ministries, such as provided by New Brunswick Theological Seminary, New Brunswick, NJ 08901-1159.

Programs in developing new church plants are available, such as by Center for New Church Development, Columbia Theological Seminary, Decatur, GA 30031.

Applying Servant Leadership

Armstrong, Richard S. *Service Evangelism*. Philadelphia: Westminster, 1979.

_____. Trilogy on eight areas of ministry: *The Pastor as Evangelist*, 1984. *The Pastor-Evangelist in Worship*, 1986. *The Pastor-Evangelist in the Parish*, 1990. All from Louisville: Westminster John Knox.

For local church training, see *Faithful Witnesses*. Presbyterian Church USA: Congregational Ministry Division.

Manson, T. W. *Ministry and Priesthood, Christ's and Ours*. Richmond: John Knox.

Implementing Servant Leadership

Robert K. Greenleaf Center for Servant-Leadership, 921 E. 86th St., Suite 200, Indianapolis, IN 46240 (317-259-1241; www.greenleaf.org).

The Servant Leadership School, 1640 Columbia Rd. NW, Washington, D.C. 20009. Associated with Church of the Savior.

Writings on the Spiritual Life

Vanier, Jan. Founder of L'Arche Communities for the Handicapped. Contact Daybreak Publications, 11339 Yonge St., Richmond Hill, ON L4C 4X7, Canada.

Weavings: A Journal of the Christian Spiritual Life. 1908 Grand Ave., P.O. Box 851, Nashville, TN 37202-9808.

Scripture Index

The Author

David S. Young is a pastor, professor, and friend. He has served a number of congregations in regular and interim pastorates. Currently he serves as interim pastor of the Mohler Church of the Brethren near Ephrata, Pennsylvania.

While he was taking a doctor of ministry program in church renewal, he adopted the style of servant leadership. He has become an appreciated teacher in seminaries. In 1986 he began teaching intensive courses on servant leadership and church renewal at Eastern Baptist Theological Seminary. He has also taught at Eastern Mennonite, Bethany Theological, and Princeton Theological seminaries.

Young has a passion for the spiritual life of the church. He has discovered how the spiritual track can lead to a constructive process of discerning dynamics of renewal from a Scripture text, identifying strengths of a congregation, and learning biblical traits of servant leaders. With such preparation, churches can design and implement a three-year plan of ministry and renewal.

Central to such renewal is leadership, and David was invited to extend his teaching to this topic. Servant leadership is a key topic for renewal, and the style of the servant leader is deeply rooted biblically. In this book the author describes characteristics of servant leadership and how it can effect renewal in the local church.

Young has a keen interest in the handicapped. He appreciates the learning style utilized for the mentally challenged and identifies the servant as one who feels drawn by the divine will to serve God and others. Many pastors and church leaders live out this model, and their experiences are shared in this book.

David and his wife, Joan Elizabeth, are members of the Drexel Hill Church of the Brethren. They have two grown sons.